D1491004

THE ART OF
SMART
FOOTBALL

THE ART OF SMART FOOTBALL

CHRIS B. BROWN

Copyright © 2015 Chris B. Brown
All rights reserved.

No part of this book may be reproduced, or stored in a retrieval system, or
transmitted in any form or by any means, electronic, mechanical, photocopying,
recording, or otherwise, without express written permission of the publisher.

ISBN: 069244825X
ISBN 13: 9780692448250

DEDICATION

To my daughter Catherine, who makes every day beautiful.

TABLE OF CONTENTS

Omnia mutantur, nihil interit. (Everything changes, nothing perishes.)

—Ovid

INTRODUCTION

Football is complex. Not complex in the same way that, say, nuclear engineering is complex, but for a sport centered around tackling the person carrying an oblong leather ball, it qualifies. So while it's easy enough to turn on a football game and marvel at quarterbacks rifling passes to receivers or running backs breaking tackles, if that's all you notice then you miss out on most of what makes football great, not to mention the actions of twenty or twenty-one other players.

And you also miss out on what makes football unique: namely, how the tactics and strategies fueling the sport—really, the nature of the game itself—are constantly evolving. No sport lends itself to planning and tactics more than football, and players and coaches spend countless hours studying opponents and brainstorming tactics, all in preparation of just a handful of games every season. The result is a sport where every assignment, every movement, and every step is designed to defeat some tactic of the opponent, which in turn sparks another tactical reaction, and the cat and mouse game goes on and on.

This book is about these strategic evolutions. But it's also about the people—the desperate coach experimenting with new tactics because he has nothing to lose, the wise old hand who has answers because he's seen it all, the great player whose skill permanently reshapes the game in his image—who are the source of this continuous, endlessly fascinating change.

WHO'S LAUGHING NOW?

Twenty years ago, Pete Carroll's name was a punch line. Following the 1994 season, the New York Jets fired Carroll after one year as head coach. It wasn't simply that Carroll's team lost; it was how it lost. The '94 Jets started 6–5 then crashed, losing their final five games in a series of lifeless performances. The collapse began with a last-second loss on one of the most famous plays in NFL history: After leading the Dolphins back from a 24–6 third-quarter deficit, Miami's Dan Marino brought his team to the line with just less than thirty seconds remaining. Marino signaled that he was going to spike the ball to stop the clock—then didn't. Instead, he rifled a touchdown pass to Mark Ingram, pushing the Dolphins to a 28–24 win. The lasting image from the Jets' 1994 season was of a motionless Carroll gazing blankly at the field as the Dolphins celebrated Marino's ruse.

Carroll got another shot at being a head coach after two seasons as a defensive coordinator, this time in New England. He lasted three years before the Patriots fired him. He then spent most of the 2000 season essentially out of football, doing some consulting and some media, and even writing a few online sports columns. Southern Cal hired Carroll as head coach in December 2000, a decision that sparked a combination of derision and apathy; Carroll, who was the Trojans' fourth choice following a frantic coaching search, is lucky the Internet commentariat wasn't as robust then as it is now.

Then something unexpected happened: Carroll started winning and kept winning. Since 2001, Carroll's college and NFL teams have posted a 133-49 record, including his Seattle Seahawks' 36-12 record since 2012.

Coaching is a hard profession. It certainly has its rewards, as skyrocketing salaries for NFL and college head coaches illustrate, but failure is the norm. Being a coach means eventually getting fired, and making a career out of coaching at all is an accomplishment. Carroll, however, has done something especially rare, pushing through wrenching public failure to succeed beyond all expectations. A coach can't do that without learning from past mistakes, and Carroll has certainly changed for the better.

Much of the credit goes to Carroll's defense, which has been the foundation of his success and remains closely tied to the first lessons he learned as a very young coach. "To be successful on defense, you need to develop a philosophy," Carroll said while still at USC. "If you don't have a clear view of your philosophy, you will be floundering all over the place. If you win, it will be pure luck."

Carroll's Seahawks, who won Super Bowl XLVIII and were a play away from repeating the feat, don't win with luck. They win by physically dominating opponents and playing championship-level defense. They also win thanks to Carroll's new spin on an old scheme.

...

After spending a year selling roofing materials in the Bay Area, Carroll got his start in coaching in 1974 as a graduate assistant at his alma mater, the University of the Pacific. His big break came in 1977, when he secured a GA job at the University of Arkansas under new head coach Lou Holtz and defensive co-ordinator Monte Kiffin. Carroll later called that job "the best thing that ever happened" to him.

Most graduate assistants simply want to break into coaching; Carroll got that, but he also got something else: an ideology. "I am an example of a person who got zeroed into a philosophy early," said Carroll. "Monte ran what is known in coaching circles as the 4–3 Under defense... That was the first time I started to get hold of something that had a philosophy to it. I started to grow with the defense."

Taken literally, 4-3 Under refers to a particular personnel grouping—four defensive linemen and three linebackers (hence "4–3"), and by extension four defensive backs— where the defensive linemen align away from the offense's strong side (hence "Under") while the strong-side linebacker positions himself on the line, usually right across from the tight end. This is the same structure Kiffin ran while working for Tony Dungy and the Tampa Bay Buccaneers, and the Under front remains popular in the NFL today.

Carroll has never exclusively relied on this scheme; instead, he viewed Kiffin's 4-3 Under less as a particular alignment and more as a belief system about football. "I have been running that same base defense since 1977 when I learned it from [Kiffin]," Carroll has explained. "I have used variations of this defense my entire career. I have stayed with its principles through all my years of coaching." And the overarching principle is simple: be aggressive.

The key to being aggressive is something called "one-gapping." "There are really two [defensive] philosophies in pro football," former Tampa Bay and Indianapolis head coach (and 4–3 Under guru) Dungy said at a lecture for coaches. "Do you want to be a one-gap team or a two-gap team?" Used this way, "gap" simply refers to the space between offensive linemen, and "run fits" is coach patois for how a team handles those gaps.

The need to choose between one-gapping and two-gapping arises, according to Dungy, "because of simple math: you have eight gaps to fill, and you only have seven front players." A one-gap technique is much like it sounds. Each defender is responsible for attacking and controlling his assigned gap. By contrast, a two-gapping defender is responsible for the gaps on either side of the lineman across from him. How? He controls both gaps by controlling the blocker in between. A one-gapper attacks gaps, while a two-gapper attacks people.

Carroll, like Dungy, prefers not to two-gap. The problem isn't the theory—a potential two for one, where a single defender can clog up two running lanes, is a great deal for the defense—but rather that two-gapping too often results in hesitant defensive linemen who try to read and react and thus fail to disrupt the offense.

"When you put a defensive lineman in a gap and tell him he has to control the gap, he can play very aggressively," Carroll explained at a lecture for coaches while at USC.

"We want to be an attacking, aggressive football team," he said at another clinic. "We don't want to sit and read the play like you often have to with two-gap principles of play."

Of course, that doesn't address Dungy's math problem: the unaccounted-for eighth gap. The one-gap answer is to use a safety to fill the void. "We assign everyone a gap and use an eighth man out of the secondary to cover the eighth gap," Dungy explained at the lecture. "Our system has not changed in about twenty years."

If you watch Carroll's Seattle team, you'll see all of this at work: aggressive one-gap techniques, safeties rocking down to help against the run, and that classic 4–3 Under front. But that's not all you'll see.

• • •

Sandwiched between his failed stints with the Jets and Patriots, Carroll had a successful two-year run from 1995 to 1996 coordinating a talented San Francisco 49ers defense. He coached some great players, including safeties Merton Hanks and Tim McDonald as well as linebacker (and former Seahawks and current Oakland Raiders assistant coach) Ken Norton Jr. Those players, coupled with defensive-line coach Bill McPherson's experience, allowed Carroll to experiment with new wrinkles and put together a comprehensive defense that had answers for almost anything an offense tried. Carroll told the *Seattle Times* that the defense he ran in San Francisco represented "the ultimate package."

Although Carroll used bits of that system with New England, he never got it fully up and running, and it was simply too much for college players, even the very talented ones at USC. "I was the defensive coordinator and putting the whole thing together [at USC], but our guys just couldn't handle it," said Carroll. "It was just too much stuff, and it was too much for the coaches."

Carroll's Seahawks are a different story. In Carroll's first season with Seattle, his team ranked a dreadful twenty-fifth in scoring defense and twenty-seventh in total defense. The Seahawks jumped to seventh and ninth respectively the next year and haven't looked back since, including finishing first in both categories in 2013. The biggest reason is the job Carroll and general manager John Schneider have done in revamping the roster. Not far behind, however, is the implementation of new wrinkles to Carroll's base defensive system, with many pulled from his days in San Francisco.

Specifically, Carroll often calls for at least one defensive lineman to two-gap in an effort to get the best of both worlds: with one or two linemen two-gapping to clog additional running lanes, the remaining defenders are free to attack their gaps or drop into pass coverage. Hybrid defenses that can steal back a gap have become increasingly necessary as modern offenses tilt the arithmetic in their favor by using the quarterback as a running threat in the read-option.

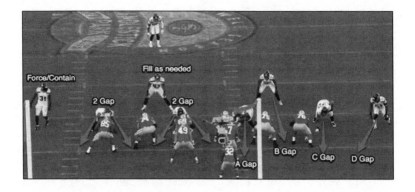

In addition to Carroll's tactics, the Seahawks' personnel dictate changes. Seattle's defense is talented, but it's also rather eclectic: Tall and skinny, short and stout, Seattle's defenders come in all shapes and sizes. As just one example, in 2013 the Seahawks started 254-pound Chris Clemons at one defensive end spot and 323-pound Red Bryant at the other. But Bryant is a perfect two-gapper, and Carroll often placed him directly across from an offensive guard or tackle to blow up running plays to the offense's strong side.

While these wrinkles trace back to Carroll's previous NFL stints, he refined the art of adapting them to his talent while coaching college. "That really came out of my time at SC," Carroll told Seahawks.com. "We forced [young players] to play, in essence. And then we discovered if we asked them to do things they could do uniquely well, that they could elevate faster and find their confidence sooner."

• • •

Nowhere have Carroll's adaptations been more successful than with Seattle's pass defense, led by the so-called Legion of Boom. The unit led the NFL in every conceivable metric in 2013 and 2014, which is only surprising given how often the Seahawks use one of the oldest, most basic pass coverages in all of football: Cover 3. And they don't simply use it; they use it to shut opponents down.

Also known as three-deep zone coverage, Cover 3 is a fundamental defensive building block; almost every high school team in the country runs some version. As the name implies, three defenders drop and divide the field into three deep zones—typically the two cornerbacks on the outsides and the free safety in the middle—while four other defenders drop to defend underneath passes as the remainder rush the QB. This coverage is sound against the pass and allows an extra defender to come up to stop the run, but it's also conservative, which is why veteran NFL quarterbacks tend to carve it up, and thus why it's not commonly used in the NFL on passing downs.

All of the basic elements are there when Seattle runs Cover 3, but subtle tweaks make it deadly. Carroll often brings strong safety Kam Chancellor near the line as essentially another linebacker, while all-everything free safety Earl Thomas roams deep center field, instinctively breaking on passes or flying up to stuff the run. (Carroll is not afraid to reverse those roles, however.) While at USC, Carroll described his ideal free safety as "a natural player" that "you don't have to coach" much. Thomas is all that and more, but the real key is that Carroll keeps things simple for his star. "If you have a million reads for your secondary, you are crazy," Carroll said at a coaching clinic. "At the highest level in the NFL, the pass game is as complex as you can imagine. However, if [the free safety] can play the post and the seam routes, then they can learn to play at that level." Thomas, it's safe to say, can play the post and the seam.

As good as Seattle's safeties are, however, its cornerbacks are even more crucial, particularly former fifth-round pick and converted wide receiver Richard Sherman. Now arguably the best cover corner in the NFL, Sherman was an afterthought on every NFL team's draft board, including Seattle's.

"[Sherman]'s a guy I watched on film that we weren't even thinking about much," Carroll said. "But then I saw him playing press and tackling and knew him as a receiver coming out of high school, and thought, 'Oh boy.'"

Sherman's skills allow Carroll to put his spin on old, conservative Cover 3 zone coverage. Unlike most zones, Seattle's cornerbacks play tight press coverage on the outside wide receivers as long as a receiver's initial steps are straight downfield.

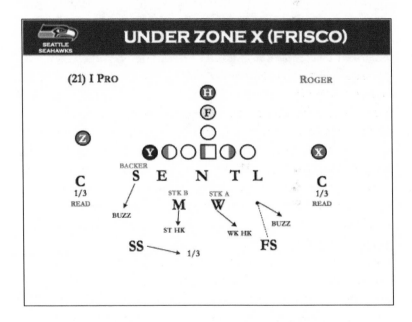

Carroll's defense provides all of the benefits of traditional Cover 3—namely a deep middle safety and excellent run support—without conceding easy throws. Cover 3 is as old as the forward pass, but Carroll's Seahawks have made it modern by making it their own. And the result has been the best pass defense in the NFL in more than a decade.

. . .

The Carroll who coached the Jets and Patriots wouldn't have been able to build and maintain the kind of team he now has in Seattle. He had the schemes, but he hadn't yet mastered their application. Carroll has evolved over time by turning earlier failures into lessons.

Interestingly, Carroll's own description of this evolution is somewhat paradoxical: "There is no offensive-play calling or defensive scheme that is going to win championships for you. It is how you can adapt and adjust to making the schemes work. *The only way you can do that is to have a strong belief system.*" (emphasis mine)

That explanation might only make sense to Carroll, a man who counts both John Wooden and Jerry Garcia among his primary influences. Carroll thinks his unshakable belief in those early lessons from Holtz and Kiffin have enabled him to evolve those ideas and adapt them to the present, and most important, to improve as a coach. In the spirit of that seeming paradox, here's one of my own: Pete Carroll, the coach who succeeded through failing.

CREATING THE NEW JOE COOL

When Green Bay Packers head coach Mike McCarthy began his first NFL job in 1993, as a Kansas City Chiefs offensive assistant working with quarterbacks, he immediately inherited a rather tricky assignment: coaching Joe Montana.

McCarthy had gone to KC to work with his mentor, Paul Hackett, the Chiefs' new offensive coordinator and a former assistant for Bill Walsh's San Francisco 49ers. While working together at the University of Pittsburgh, Hackett and McCarthy had installed a version of Walsh's legendary West Coast offense, which had powered four Super Bowl titles in the 1980s. McCarthy became enamored of the system during those years with the Panthers, immersing himself in the offense that was taking over football. By the time he went to the Chiefs, McCarthy felt he was ready for any challenge.

Well, almost any challenge: prior to the 1993 season, the Chiefs traded for Montana, the veteran quarterback with extensive West Coast offense experience and the man Jerry Rice referred to as "God." McCarthy told Milwaukee's *Journal*

Sentinel that the gravity of the assignment didn't register until he excitedly let some of his close friends know that he'd be coaching Montana, and one responded by asking, "What in the [expletive] are you going to teach Joe Montana?" It was a good question, and it led McCarthy to become as much Montana's student as his teacher, soaking in all the knowledge he could from the future Hall of Famer.

More than twenty years later, on the brink of a divisional-round playoff game against the Dallas Cowboys, McCarthy again finds himself in a teacher-student partnership with an elite pupil: Packers quarterback Aaron Rodgers. Though McCarthy is facing a similar challenge of figuring out how to help one of the game's best quarterbacks get even better, his relationship with Rodgers is far more collaborative than his pairing with Montana ever was, allowing coach and quarterback to try to improve themselves, each other, and the very offense Walsh taught Montana so long ago.

• • •

At some point, the story of every great quarterback morphs from anecdote to myth, and Rodgers's narrative fits the mold. Barely recruited out of high school, Rodgers wound up at Butte Community College, where Cal coach Jeff Tedford (while scouting a tight end) noticed a skinny QB running around making accurate throws and offered him a spot with the Golden Bears.

Under Tedford's tutelage, Rodgers vaulted from unknown passer to surefire first-rounder, wowing pro scouts by tying an NCAA record with twenty-three consecutive completions in a near road upset of top-ranked Southern Cal, a team loaded with future NFL stars (and coached by some guy named Pete Carroll). Rodgers looked like the potential first overall NFL draft pick, but he fell to number twenty-four, where the Packers selected him as Brett Favre's heir apparent. Favre, of course, was uninterested in mentoring his replacement, famously telling ESPN, "My contract doesn't say I have to get Aaron Rodgers ready to play...I'm not obligated one bit to help anyone."

It was an inauspicious start for a young quarterback, but Rodgers credits his early years as being crucial to his development. Though the player Rodgers is today stems primarily from his talent and work ethic, being a successful NFL quarterback requires luck as well as skill, and being lucky usually means getting to work with the right people. When the Packers fired Mike Sherman and hired McCarthy as head coach after Rodgers's first season, it altered the direction of both McCarthy's and Rodgers's careers.

McCarthy was hardly a slam-dunk hire. Prior to Green Bay, he had coached relatively pedestrian offenses in New Orleans from 2000 to 2004, and had spent the 2005 season as offensive coordinator for the 49ers, a 4–12 team that finished a woeful thirtieth in the league in scoring and thirty-second in total yards. But Packers general manager Ted Thompson brought him in hoping the coach's deep knowledge of the West Coast offense and renowned touch with quarterbacks would tame Favre after a 29-interception season, while also developing Favre's anointed replacement. Though Favre bounced back under McCarthy, throwing for 4,155 yards, 28 touchdowns, and only 15 interceptions in 2007 en route to the NFC title game, he began to threaten retirement, and by 2008 Thompson and the organization were ready to switch to Rodgers, convinced after witnessing his dramatic improvement that the QB had the makings of a future star.

Since his days as an assistant under Hackett at Pitt, McCarthy has run a QB school every offseason, where, away from the pressure of preparing for a weekly opponent, McCarthy can teach his quarterbacks the finer points of the position. In addition to extensive drill work, McCarthy often gives his quarterbacks lengthy written tests, once even asking his non-Montana quarterbacks in Kansas City to write an essay describing the Chiefs' version of the West Coast offense "from a philosophical perspective."

Rodgers has clearly benefited from McCarthy's training. As good of a prospect as Rodgers was coming out of Cal, it's striking how different he looks now: he's more athletic, more natural, and has a stronger arm. While primary credit goes to the long hours Rodgers spends developing his craft on his own, McCarthy provided a structure for that process.

Specifically, when Rodgers arrived in the NFL, there was what McCarthy has labeled a "stiffness" to his game. Under McCarthy's tutelage, that has since melted away to reveal the fluid, smooth quarterback we see today. Tedford, Rodgers's college coach and a current CFL head man, is an excellent quarterback teacher, but his college passers tended to be a bit robotic: they all dropped back, held the ball, and released it the same way. That made sense for raw high school and junior college passers, who had to quickly learn the fine points of quarterbacking in order to execute Tedford's pro-style attack, but great NFL passers must make their fundamentals serve them, not the other way around.

The most obvious example of Rodgers making this shift is how he holds the ball. He used to hold the ball up near his ear while in the pocket, on the theory that it cut down on the time he had to bring the ball back before throwing it forward. Under McCarthy and Packers quarterback coach/offensive coordinator Tom Clements, however, Rodgers gradually began holding the ball between the middle of his chest and his throwing shoulder, a more natural spot that keeps his throwing motion compact while allowing him to rotate his body just enough to create extra velocity.

More subtly, Rodgers has improved his accuracy, which might sound crazy when discussing a guy who once completed 23 passes in a row in college. But in the NFL, accuracy must be an every-snap thing, particularly in the West Coast offense. Walsh used to jump all over Montana and Steve Young if they missed the precise spot he wanted on a given play—the upper right corner of a receiver's jersey, a receiver's left eye, etc. For Rodgers, the key to improved accuracy was perfecting his footwork. "Learning to time up my drop with each route has been a big thing with me," Rodgers told *ESPN The Magazine* in 2011. That didn't just mean opting for a three-step drop versus a five-step drop, but instead learning that while a hitch route might require a three-step drop with one big and two quick steps, a slant route might benefit from three big steps. Rodgers said that mastering those nuances for every conceivable route allows him "to throw the ball in rhythm and hit the same release point with every throw, meaning that no matter what else is happening, the ball comes out on a similar plane. That's when accuracy comes."

Indeed, Rodgers is the most visceral of today's great quarterbacks, oscillating effortlessly between quick timing passes and lasers thrown while on the move after being flushed from the pocket. He often reminds me less of a traditional quarterback than of a great jump shooter in basketball who can hit a shot falling sideways and out of bounds because he always maintains perfect upper-body form. But the real fun comes from watching Rodgers operate the Packers' modernized West Coast offense, a system perfectly tailored to his quick release and even quicker mind.

• • •

The offense Rodgers operates in Green Bay is based on the same ideas, concepts, and even specific plays that Hackett, McCarthy, and Montana used in Kansas City and that Montana and Hackett had run with the 49ers, all of which are rooted in Walsh's West Coast offense. While most people think of short timing passes when they hear the term "West Coast offense," Walsh's coaching tree—and the coaching tree of his coaching tree—is so long because his insights extended beyond well-designed pass plays to encompass a uniquely thorough, detailed approach to game planning, analyzing defensive weaknesses, and teaching and developing players. Those precepts are Walsh's true legacy, and they now fuel the Packers' offensive success.

In McCarthy's early years, he immersed himself in Walsh's ideas and language—22 Z-In, 2 Jet X-Sluggo Seam, and so on. But rather than adhering religiously to those lessons, McCarthy and Rodgers have crafted a version of Walsh's offense that constantly evolves to keep pace with a changing game. McCarthy once told *USA Today*, "Football is a cycle. You're going to see things in this league or out of this league and in college football. It's very important to stay on the front side of that cycle." The Packers' offense may be rooted in the playbook McCarthy learned from Hackett twenty-plus years ago, but it works because he and Rodgers have subtly blended in new-school tactics.

While the West Coast offense dominated the NFL in the 1990s and early 2000s, it has increasingly fallen out of favor because its emphasis on precision and preparation has too often translated into inflexibility and needless complexity. The traditional West Coast offense features a seemingly countless number of plays—former Packers coach Mike Holmgren once said his playbook contained at least fifteen hundred plays—because on each play, each player had a specific job, such as running a post or a slant. As a result, the only way to take advantage of a shifting, evolving defense was to add yet another new play and hope to call it at the right time, in what amounted to an impossibly hard game of rock-paper-scissors.

That's not a feasible approach against modern, malleable defenses, and with Rodgers under center, it's also not necessary. For example, one of the Packers' most productive pass plays is "three verticals," in which Green Bay's receivers have the option to change their routes based on the coverage, trusting Rodgers to see their adjustments in real time.

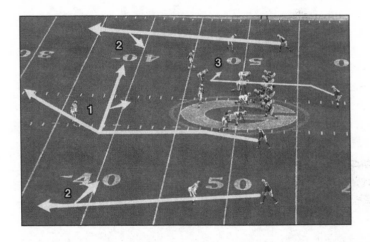

On this play against the Panthers in 2014, both of Green Bay's outside receivers, Jordy Nelson and Davante Adams, can run either straight down the field on "go" routes (as Nelson does to Rodgers's right) or stop after 12–15 yards if the defender is playing soft coverage (as Adams ultimately did on the play). Meanwhile, the slot receiver, Randall Cobb, runs a "middle read": if the defense plays with two safeties deep, Cobb will split the safeties and run deep down the middle, but if there's a deep middle safety like on this play, he'll turn his route into a square-in and break across the field into Rodgers's vision.

While this play, which the Packers run over and over again, requires Rodgers and his receivers to all be on the same page—and requires Rodgers to process all of this information and make an accurate throw in fractions of a second—it also replaces in one shot as many as ten different plays from the traditional West Coast offense.

This idea of multiple concepts within each play flows through Green Bay's offense. In Favre and in Rodgers's early seasons, this typically meant combining multiple pass concepts within the same play and letting the QB pick the side based on the defense. More recently, however, the Packers have made extensive use of "packaged plays" that combine run blocking from the offensive line with screens or downfield passes by the receivers, while the QB has the option to hand off to a running back or throw downfield.

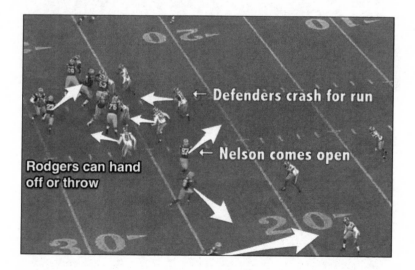

Under McCarthy, Green Bay was among the first NFL teams to begin using packaged plays, which first began bubbling up in college football roughly five years ago. (McCarthy has several friends coaching college on whom he leans for new ideas, including Kevin Sumlin, the forward-thinking coach at Texas A&M.) The above diagram shows an inside running play—complete with linemen run blocking—married with a quick "pop" or seam route by receiver Jordy Nelson. This concept is a beautifully simple way to keep defenses honest if they try to crash down on running back Eddie Lacy and Green Bay's increasingly productive run game. It's also a way for the Packers to use Rodgers's quick decision-making ability without putting him in harm's way.

But the Packers' success doesn't stem solely from their ability to embrace the latest and greatest; while Green Bay excels at innovating, it's also better than any other NFL team at executing many of the same plays Walsh used with Montana, most notably the slant pass. Hard as it is to believe, few NFL teams consistently throw the quick slant anymore, as most have replaced it with skinny posts or quick square-ins or stopped bothering altogether.

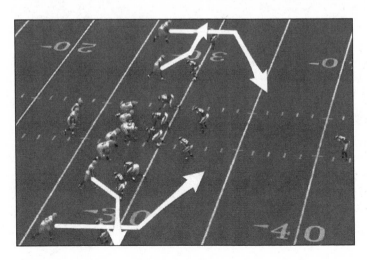

Put on a Packers game, though, and it can feel like watching old 49ers game film. It's not uncommon for Rodgers to complete five to ten slant passes in a game—he likes them against soft coverage because they give him easy access, and he loves them against the blitz. When New England tried to bring pressure on Rodgers late in the half in a game in 2014, he checked into a basic slant to Nelson and, forty-five yards later, Green Bay had scored.

· · ·

The most famous Joe Montana anecdote so perfectly meshes with his reputation as "Joe Cool" that it seems more written than real: Standing around during a TV timeout, with the ball on the 49ers' own eight-yard line and his team down three points to the Cincinnati Bengals in Super Bowl XXIII, Montana saw that his teammates, including lineman Harris Barton, had tensed up. Then, out of the corner of his eye, he spotted something else. "There, in the stands," he said to Barton. "Isn't that John Candy?" His teammates immediately relaxed, Montana marched them down the field for the game-winning touchdown, and his legend grew. Great quarterbacks come in different flavors, but the preternaturally relaxed field general is an archetype as old as football itself.

Rodgers is a few Super Bowls shy of earning direct comparisons to Montana, but—particularly compared to Peyton Manning's manic nerdiness and Tom Brady's increasingly expressive sideline demeanor—he's the closest thing we have to a modern-day Joe Cool. In 2014 alone, Rodgers pointedly told Packers fans to "R-E-L-A-X" after a loss, and on one of the most remarkable plays I've ever seen, calmly threw a game-winning touchdown pass without even bothering to buckle his chin strap.

By all accounts, Rodgers has always been this way. At a coaching clinic in 2011, Tedford recalled that, before the aforementioned crucial game against USC, Rodgers "was just walking around in the locker room with a smile on his face and getting [his teammates] going, but also getting them relaxed. He was not going haywire and yelling and screaming. He had this confidence about himself, and his leadership ability was unbelievable."

Of course, similarities in demeanor between Rodgers and Montana wouldn't matter if the two weren't also so similar on the field. "When I think about fundamental quarterback play, I think of Aaron and Joe Montana," McCarthy has said. "The productivity is obviously there, but just the way they play the position—their footwork, the balance, the athletic ability, the accuracy of the football, the vision." I see it too. Montana's gifts were his accuracy, his decision-making, and his feet, and Rodgers boasts those same attributes—plus a stronger arm.

Rodgers's talent, drive, and approach to mastering the hardest position in sports have gotten him to this point, but so has his collaboration with McCarthy. I'd be surprised if Green Bay's coach and quarterback didn't win a second Super Bowl, but they've already taken the Packers, the old West Coast offense, and the quarterback position into the modern age.

THE LONG-BALL LEGACY OF AL DAVIS

Prior to his passing in the fall of 2011, it became easy (and sometimes even appropriate) to mock Al Davis and his beloved Oakland Raiders. From poor on-field results to questionable personnel moves to Davis's never-ending quest to find a modern "Mad Bomber" at QB, the last few years of Davis's tenure were rife with issues. And nothing, perhaps, was uglier than the Raiders' ill-fated selection of quarterback JaMarcus Russell with the first overall pick of the 2007 NFL draft. Russell, whom Davis reportedly decided to draft after watching his bowl game on TV, had a strong arm, but he ate and sipped "syrup" until he became persona non grata in the NFL. But none of that should overshadow what Davis built and also what he left behind, even if at the end he seemed to be grasping at the shadows of the Raiders' past success. Among his greatest contributions is also among his least well understood: the vaunted Raiders "vertical passing game."

Davis picked up the aerial bug from passing-game guru Sid Gillman when he was one of Gillman's assistants with the San Diego Chargers in the 1960s. Gillman introduced several innovations to modern football, the first of which was a timing-based approach to throwing the football. Gillman preached meticulous practice to sync the timing between quarterback and receiver, or more precisely, between the quarterback's drop back and his receiver's route. If the quarterback took a five-step drop, the primary receiver had to run his route based on a precise number of steps, such that the quarterback would throw the ball before the receiver had turned to look for it. The secondary receiver in the quarterback's progression ran his route a split second after the first receiver so that the quarterback could look for the first receiver, reset his feet, then look for the second, and still throw before that receiver turned to look for the pass. Nowadays, this emphasis on timing is so universal—in theory, if not entirely in practice—that it's difficult to believe how influential Gillman was in establishing it.

His second insight was a deeper understanding of pass defenses and how to defeat them. Defeating a man-to-man defense, then as now, is about identifying a receiver who can get open versus a particular defender. Zones, on the other hand, require more thought. Gillman realized that the key to defeating zones was spacing between receivers; if a defense had only four underneath defenders, then five receivers—even five inanimate objects with proper spacing between them—are uncoverable. The defenders are outnumbered. Thus, the idea of the zone "stretch" was born.

When Davis left Gillman's staff he took Sid's playbook—and, more importantly, his ideas—with him. But Davis wasn't content to stretch the field horizontally; he wanted to get vertical. If Gillman could get an inert object open against a zone, Davis tested how he'd do if he added his favorite ingredient: speed. Gillman, of course, used vertical stretches—passing concepts that spaced receivers not left to right, but deep to short—but for Davis they became the centerpiece of his offense. Indeed, this is what Davis meant when he brought the vertical game to Oakland. It was not a matter of throwing deep bombs for their own sake (though sometimes it was that too) but was instead the science of stretching defenses to their breaking point. With receivers at varying depths, a small defensive error often meant a fifteen-yard pass play for Davis's offense, and a serious mistake meant a touchdown.

Davis continued to tweak the Gillman offense by adding more formations, adding options for running backs in the passing game, and generally expanding the possibilities of what an offense could do with the football. This was innovative stuff, so much so that it had an outsize effect on a young Raiders assistant coach by the name of Bill Walsh, who went on to craft his own multi Super Bowl winning offense with the 49ers that looked a lot like what Davis had created in Oakland. As Walsh explained in his book *Building a Champion*:

> [Al Davis]'s pass offense included an almost unlimited variety of pass patterns as well as a system of calling them and utilized the backs and tight ends much more extensively than other offenses....To develop an understanding of it took time, but once learned, it was invaluable.

This is not the description of the Al Davis offense you usually see—as some kind of simplistic, backyard "heave it up" strategy. Al Davis's vertical game was, in short, built on stretching the defense vertically while using all available receivers—deep, intermediate, and short—to take what the defense gave up anywhere on the field. It's not Al's fault that defenses often yielded big plays to the Raiders.

In Davis's offense, as is the case today, the ultimate vertical-stretch passes are true flood or three-level vertical stretches, with one receiver deep, another at an intermediate depth, and a third short. Pass defenses generally have only two layers of defenders—deep safeties and underneath coverage players—so when there are receivers at three depths, it is extremely difficult to cover them all. For example, Davis's early Raiders teams often used the "strong-side flood" route, a pass concept still popular today.

On the play, an outside receiver runs a go route straight upfield, trying to beat his defender deep and otherwise taking the coverage with him. An inside receiver (here the tight end) runs a corner route at fifteen yards, breaking to the sideline while an underneath receiver (here the running back) runs to the flat. On the back side, the outside receiver runs a post route as an alert for the quarterback. He's not the primary read, but if the deep defenders overreact to the three receivers to the right, the home-run shot is always available. Because the defense has only two defenders (the corner and the safety) to cover three receivers, it shouldn't be able to defend the play. Al's secret—and it is the same secret Gillman discovered and Walsh extended—is that the surest way to hit those deep passes is to consistently hit the underneath ones.

These vertical-stretch passes help explain why Davis became obsessed with speed. Obviously, speed gives a vertical receiver a chance to get deep, but even if he does not actually get open, he still stretches the defense, thus opening up the entire field. Speed distorts defenses, forcing them to cover wider swaths of the field, exposing the weak defenders and the voids around them. If Davis could have a receiver like Warren Wells, who in 1969 totaled 1,260 yards on only 47 catches for the Raiders—a staggering 26.8 yards per completion—then his other receivers would have plenty of room to roam.

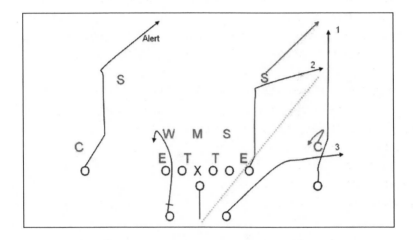

And yet while Davis may have been hooked on speed and the vertical game, those addictions alone weren't responsible for the Raiders' struggles in his later years. The Raiders were derailed by weaknesses at the two most important positions for implementing Davis's vision as owner: head coach and quarterback. Throughout the 1970s, Davis had John Madden, a coach who could make Raiders football a reality. And for more than a decade Oakland had two quarterbacks, Daryle the "Mad Bomber" Lamonica and Ken the "Snake" Stabler, who could execute the sophisticated vertical passing game the way Davis wanted.

But long after Madden, Lamonica, and Stabler left the Raiders, Davis remained. As the years went on, Davis couldn't expect his coaches to run the offense exactly as he'd taught it to Bill Walsh—nor did he want them to. But he always knew how he wanted it to look, and at times the Raiders achieved something close to the excellence that had once been the norm. In football, great teams and great organizations exist only in the moments before the next signing season or injury or retirement, or even the next death. It's not reasonable to expect what Davis accomplished early in his Raiders career to continue into perpetuity. But, despite whatever bitterness or decay emanated from the Raiders in Davis's last years, the fact remains that he gave all of us more than we gave him. Davis didn't just mold his football team and his coaches and his players in his image—he molded the game itself.

CONTROLLED CHAOS:
ZONE BLITZING AND THE EVOLUTION OF
PATTERN-MATCH COVERAGES

The word "blitz" is maybe the most exciting word in football. Like a football Mexican standoff, it conjures up the ultimate him-or-me scenario—a mass of defenders in single-minded blind pursuit of the quarterback and an offense that knows it might be only a missed tackle away from a long touchdown. Former Florida State football coach Bobby Bowden once gave a clinic lecture about the blitz aptly (and neutrally) titled, "Hang Loose—One of Us Is Fixin' to Score." A blitz is the closest thing we have to football bedlam.

But a zone blitz isn't quite bedlam, as it combines the aggressiveness of a man-to-man blitz with more conservative zone coverage behind it. Zone blitzes are not particularly new, but while the blitz element continues to receive the most attention, it's the continuing changes in the coverage behind it that make zone blitzes the most important defensive tactic in modern football.

In the mid-1980s, defenses across the NFL faced a common problem: how to stop the precision-passing offenses becoming so prevalent throughout the league. Most notably, it was how to stop the San Francisco 49ers, led by resident NFL offensive genius Bill Walsh. Walsh had studied the passing game under some of the game's masters—Paul Brown, Sid Gillman, and Al Davis—but had taken the next step by planning every detail, every subtle movement by the quarterback, offensive line, and receiver. Walsh transformed passing from a combustible, high-risk–high-reward strategy into something certain and predictable. His quarterbacks completed a higher percentage of their passes, didn't throw interceptions, and didn't take sacks. He'd kept the reward and reduced the risk, and defenses needed an answer, fast.

Walsh's protégés were hired around the league. One of them, offensive assistant Sam Wyche, became head coach of the Bengals, and upon his arrival he enlisted Cincinnati defensive-backs coach Dick LeBeau as his new defensive coordinator. As Tim Layden explains in his book, *Blood, Sweat and Chalk*, LeBeau had experimented with the idea of combining a blitz with zone coverage prior to Wyche's arrival, and when the new head coach endorsed the idea, the zone blitz became LeBeau's focus as a defensive coordinator.

For advice, he traveled to Baton Rouge to meet with Louisiana State University head coach Bill Arnsparger, a well-known defensive guru. Before he got to LSU, Arnsparger coached some of the NFL's greatest defenses, first with the Baltimore Colts in the 1960s and later the Miami Dolphins—both teams led by Don Shula. He and Arnsparger won two Super Bowls in Miami, where Arnsparger coordinated the famed No-Name

Defense. One of those Dolphins defenders—he, in fact, had a name: Bob Matheson—was a linebacker whom Arnsparger began using as a defensive end and in their 4–3 scheme. Together, Matheson and Arnsparger sparked two of football's most enduring defensive tactics: the 3–4 defense and, maybe even more important, the zone blitz.

"With Bob there with linebacking skills," Arnsparger told Layden, "we were able to rush five guys and cover with six. That's what you need to run a zone blitz." Arnsparger continued to develop the zone blitz through the early 1980s, later relying on converted linebacker Kim Bokamper as the versatile defensive lineman who could drop into coverage. By the time he left for Baton Rouge—and long before he would coordinate a defense in his sixth Super Bowl, this time with the San Diego Chargers—Arnsparger had refined his theory of the zone blitz. As he explained in his book, *Coaching Defensive Football*:

> What makes the zone blitz successful is that it allows the defense to bring outside linebackers and safeties to one side or both sides without using man-to-man blitz coverage. Normal blitzes use man-to-man coverage. The offensive line and one or two backs are assigned to block the defensive line and linebackers. In the zone blitz, the linebacker blitzes along with a secondary player, but the offensive pickup is different. It is different because defensive linemen who usually rush are now dropping out to short inside zones to replace the linebacker and secondary player that blitz. Because of the blitzer's path, it is difficult for the offensive linemen to adjust.

LeBeau had clearly come to the right man. Not only was Arnsparger employing the types of tactics at the college level that LeBeau wanted to bring to the pros, but—true to form—Arnsparger had thought through the theory behind the tactic as well. "Bill's catchphrase was that he wanted to get 'safe pressure,' on the quarterback," LeBeau told Layden. "And that expression stuck with me because that was a very succinct way to summarize exactly what I was looking for. Safe pressure. I walked out the door saying those words to myself."

Like Arnsparger, LeBeau has had his strategies vindicated by his success. To go with his Super Bowl rings and the success of his own protégés, LeBeau is a member of the NFL Hall of Fame. For the last quarter century, innovations by Arnsparger and LeBeau have been the one counter to a football world full of would-be Bill Walshes determined to show off their offensive genius. Today, the zone blitz is ubiquitous, and the accolades recently—and rightly—afforded to LeBeau confirm what many already know.

· · ·

LeBeau's trip to the bayou is only half the story. The other half comes from about fifteen years ago. Unsurprisingly, those would-be Bill Walshes—and even Bill Walsh himself, to some extent—did not simply concede defeat to LeBeau's newest tactic. Instead, offenses tried to find ways to counteract it. "I always felt that we contributed greatly to the development of the run-and-shoot offense," said LeBeau. "Teams were just looking for quicker and quicker ways to attack, to the point where it might not even matter where the pressure was coming from." He's right. The run-and-shoot offense, as well as later iterations of spread offenses, arose in a world replete with zone blitzes, and much of their design centered on identifying and exploiting any weaknesses those blitzes left.

The biggest of those weaknesses came from what was originally a strength—the zone coverage behind the blitz. Many of the earliest zone blitzes Arnsparger called in Miami were not actually blitzes as we think of them now. The Dolphins would rush only four players in total, simply swapping out a rushing linebacker for a zone-dropping defensive lineman. As a result, these defenses were just as sound against the pass as the zone defenses that had been run for the past fifty or so years. Defenders dropped to a spot, watched for a receiver in that area, and broke on the ball as it was released. Even with the threat of blitzes, quarterbacks eventually started exploiting the many soft spots on the field.

Nick Saban, currently the head coach at Alabama, was the defensive coordinator under Bill Belichick when the two were with the Cleveland Browns in the early 1990s. Saban has succinctly summed up the early problems of traditional spot-dropping zone coverages: "Well, when Marino's throwing it, that old break-on-the-ball shit don't work."

The answer that Saban, Belichick and others developed was "pattern-match" coverage—essentially man coverage that uses zone principles to identify the matchups. As Saban explained in a lecture to high school coaches:

You can play coverages in three ways. You can play zone, man, or pattern-match man. Pattern-match man is a coverage that plays the pattern after the pattern distribution. That means you pick up in man coverage after the receivers make their initial breaks and cuts. We number receivers from the outside going inside. If the number-one receiver crosses with the number-two receiver, we do not pick up the man coverage until they define where they are going.

In other words, the zone blitz had come full circle. What began as a way to blitz without playing man coverage had started incorporating man coverage all over again, this time in an entirely new way.

Using pattern-match principles allowed defenses to overcome the deficiencies in both the manic, risk-heavy man-to-man blitzes and the easy-to-exploit soft spots in the zone-coverage scheme. There was now a way to keep the safety of the zone and the tighter coverage of man-to-man. Defenses had finally done for blitzing what Walsh had done for passing—keeping the reward but eliminating the risk.

The nuances of a pattern-match zone blitz are, as one would guess, rather extensive, but the principle is simple. "I had the opportunity to work for [New York Giants defensive coordinator] Steve Spagnuolo," said Florida International University defensive coordinator Matt House. "He had a great analogy talking about zone pressure. He said, 'All you do is roll out the basketball and tell the players to play three-on-three.' The players will talk, communicate, and switch on the picks. We do the same thing in zone blitz coverage."

The most common modern zone blitz is the "fire zone," a five-man blitz behind which the defense plays coverage with three defenders deep and three underneath. The only limit to the countless arrangements of the five blitzers is a defensive coordinator's creativity, but the coverage assignments are more finite.

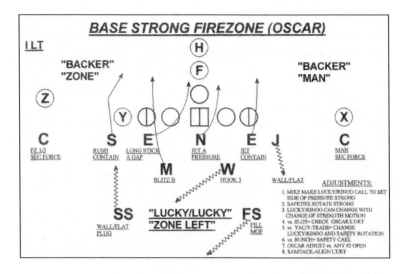

The three deep defenders divide the field into thirds, with the cornerbacks effectively playing the outside receivers—the first receivers from the sideline—on any downfield routes. Were these outside receivers to run immediately to the inside, however, such as on a shallow crossing route, the corner would make an "under" call and play his deep third zone like a traditional zone player. If that outside receiver moves far enough inside to become the innermost receiver in the pattern distribution, he becomes the middle linebacker's responsibility, a coverage known as "number three."

The most interesting assignment goes to the outside, underneath defenders, labeled in the diagram as "SCF/seam" but also known in the NFL as "Bronco" coverage players. ("SCF" stands for "seam-curl-flat," which is the order of priorities for these defenders.) These are the true pattern-match players, and they have the toughest job. It's their responsibility to determine whether the play is man, zone, or some combination thereof, all based on what is most favorable to the defense.

Fire zones are three-deep coverages, and offenses have known how to attack three-deep coverages for years. There are two common methods of doing so. The first is sending four receivers vertical, with the idea being that three defenders shouldn't be able to play four vertical receivers. The second is sending the outside receiver vertical while the tight end or slot runs a deep out or a curl/flat combination. The pattern-match fire zone, therefore, is specifically designed to handle these tactics. Broadly speaking, these "SCF" or "Bronco" defenders will play man-to-man on the second receiver from the sideline so long as he runs vertically down the seam or runs a deep out of any kind. If the receiver breaks hard to the inside, the SCF/Bronco defender passes him off to the inside defenders and looks for another receiver coming through his zone.

The upshot of pattern-match zone blitzes is that when executed correctly, they are the best of all possible worlds. The defense plays zone coverage against pass patterns designed to beat man-to-man coverage against pass patterns—all verticals—designed to defeat zones.

The pattern-match zone blitz is not a magic bullet that solves any problem a dynamic offense might present. Every scheme has its strengths and weaknesses, and it's still up to the players to bring the diagrams to life. But blitzing is as old as football itself, and as long as QBs like Aaron Rodgers, Tom Brady, and Peyton Manning are playing quarterback, to blitz, teams must cover as well.

· · ·

More than a decade after their meeting in Baton Rouge, Arnsparger, another Super Bowl appearance under his belt and now retired, visited LeBeau at the Bengals training camp in

Georgetown, Kentucky. "I watched a practice, and afterward Dick and I chatted. I thanked him for his kindness and congratulated him on developing the zone blitz to the point where it is today," wrote Arnsparger. "The scheme has grown a great deal since the beginning. Like everything in football, when you see something good, you add your ideas and make it better—and the zone blitz is no exception." Great coaches do not necessarily seek to change the game but instead are stewards for a time—for their players, for the ideas of the day, for football itself—merely doing their best to leave each better than they found it.

THE NEW ENGLAND PATRIOTS' "ERHARDT-PERKINS" OFFENSE

It's late in the first quarter. A play ends, and seconds later Tom Brady has his New England Patriots team back at the line. He gives a hand signal to his receiver, a tap to his offensive linemen. "Alabama! Alabama!" The ball is snapped. An outlet pass goes to a running back, who rumbles to the Houston forty-yard line for another first down. Subs run in. Soon the Patriots are back at the line. Except now the running back, Shane Vereen, is lined up out wide. The Texans are scrambling. Brady takes the snap and hits Vereen on a quick hitch. Vereen dips around the linebacker and spins back inside, gaining twenty-five yards before he's done.

The next play is the same play, with the same personnel, with zero time for the defense to recover. The three receivers to Brady's left crisscross around defenders while the tight end, who was lined up in the backfield, dashes to the flat. He makes the catch and takes it to Houston's one-yard line. The same eleven Patriots sprint to the line, but now it's Vereen in the backfield. The play is a run to the left, and he's into the end zone untouched. Touchdown, New England.

Since Tom Brady became the starting quarterback in New England, the Patriots have finished in the top ten in scoring thirteen times, but the way they've gotten there hasn't been nearly as consistent. In Brady's early years, Bill Belichick built his offense not around his quarterback, but rather to support him, with a steady supply of dependable receivers and a physical running game. It was when Brady moved from trusted game manager to outright star that he became the offense's centerpiece, and the need for reliable bolstering was replaced with the pursuit of a cast that could push him even further.

With a revolving supporting cast—from Corey Dillon to Wes Welker to Randy Moss to Rob Gronkowski—along with three different offensive coordinators (Charlie Weis, Josh McDaniels, and Bill O'Brien), it seems that the only constant in New England, other than Belichick and Brady, has been change. What's allowed New England to maintain its success among the shifts is that its quarterback and coach aren't the only things that have remained the same. The core of the Patriots' offensive system has been threaded through its various stages, both stabilizing the transitions and allowing the next evolution. The design and organization of New England's system is better suited than any other to adapt to an NFL game in which change—of personnel, of trends, of schemes—is the only certainty.

To an almost shocking extent, NFL offenses are homogeneous. Given that every NFL team is in, roughly speaking, the same circumstances in terms of money, resources, practice time, and facilities, this homogeneity makes some sense. After all, "football's always football," as San Diego Chargers head coach Mike McCoy said. "Everyone's running the same plays, and it's a matter of some running one concept more than another team is. It all boils down to the same thing."

· · ·

There are essentially three main offensive systems in the NFL: West Coast, Coryell, and Erhardt-Perkins. Given that every NFL team runs the same plays, each of these NFL offensive families is differentiated mostly by how those plays are communicated.

To oversimplify, the West Coast offense, made famous by Bill Walsh and still the most popular system in the NFL, uses what is essentially a memory system. On running plays, the same two-digit numbering system as most NFL and college teams is used. Passing plays, however, are typically denoted by the primary receiver's route, such as Z-In or X-Hook, while the rest of the players are required to memorize their tasks. This system is as old as football itself, which is no surprise, given that Paul Brown, Walsh's onetime mentor, is credited as much as anyone with inventing the modern conception of huddles, game plans, and play calls. For more than twenty years, this system has been the dominant one in the NFL.

The Coryell system, named after former San Diego Chargers head coach Don Coryell and used by coaches such as Norv Turner, Ernie Zampese, and Mike Martz, is built around the concept of a route tree. Many teams use a route tree (which is the idea that the base route is straight up the field, and the other routes consist of break points off that original path), but the Coryell system uses the tree as the foundation of its play-calling system. For example, the Troy Aikman–era Dallas Cowboys frequently called a play called "896," which told one outside receiver to run a square-in route (6), the tight end to run a seam straight up the field (9), and the split end to run a skinny post (8). The idea was that, using the route tree, a coach could effectively call any pass combination, and all a receiver had to know was the number associated with his route.

In recent years, as offenses and defenses have grown more complex, these systems have started crumbling under their own weight. With multiple formations and personnel groupings, calls that began as "22 Z-In" have gotten unwieldy.

In the Coryell system, the elegance of the three-digit route-tree system has been rendered almost entirely obsolete. Because NFL teams operate predominantly in one-back formations, there are often more than three players running routes, and calling any pass play means having to use both numbers and words ("896 H-Shallow F-Curl"). More critically, the numerical route-tree system gives coaches and players flexibility where they don't need it and not enough where they do. The benefit of a route-tree system is the ability to call any passing concept a coach could dream up, but that option is of very little use. Assuming the route tree has ten routes (0–9), a three-digit tree gives an offense a thousand possible route combinations. That's unnecessary. And yet, the route tree by definition only has ten possible routes, much fewer than any NFL team actually runs. This means that any other route must be called by name, thus defeating the very purpose of having a route tree.

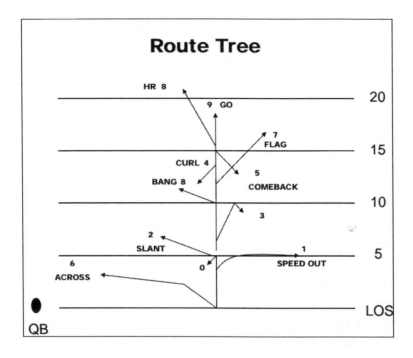

This effectively makes the Coryell system sound a lot like current West Coast offense play calls, which have no organizing principle and have morphed into monstrosities like "Scatter-2 bunch-right-zip-fire 2 jet Texas right F flat X-Q." The advantage of a play call like this is that it informs most players of their specific job better than other systems do. The disadvantage is that it's excessively clunky, and plays that are conceptually the same can have wildly different calls.

New England's offense is a member of the NFL's third offensive family, the Erhardt-Perkins system. The offense was named after the two men, Ron Erhardt and Ray Perkins, who developed it while working for the Patriots under head coach Chuck Fairbanks in the 1970s. According to Perkins, it was assembled in the same way most such systems are developed. "I don't look at it as us inventing it," he explained to the *Tuscaloosa News*. "I look at it as a bunch of coaches sitting in rooms late at night, organizing and getting things together to help players be successful."

The backbone of the Erhardt-Perkins system is that plays—pass plays in particular—are not organized by a route tree or by calling a single receiver's route, but by what coaches refer to as concepts. Each play has a name, and that name conjures up an image for both the quarterback and the other players on offense. And most important, the concept can be called from almost any formation or set. Who does what changes, but the theory and tactics driving the play do not. "In essence, you're running the same play," Perkins said. "You're just giving them some window-dressing to make it look different."

The biggest advantage of the concept-based system is that it operates from the perspective of the most critical player on offense: the quarterback. In other systems, even if the underlying principles are exactly the same, the play and its name might be very different. Rather than juggling all this information in real time, an Erhardt-Perkins quarterback only has to read a given arrangement of receivers. "You can cut down on the plays and get different looks from your formations and who's in them. It's easier for the players to learn. It's easier for the quarterback to learn," former Patriots offensive coordinator Charlie Weis told the *Boston Globe* in 2000. "You get different looks without changing his reads. You don't need an open-ended number of plays."

THREE-MAN ROUTE COMBINATION DESCRIPTIONS				
NAME	#1 RECEIVER	#2 RECEIVER	#3 RECEIVER	
2) CHOICE	12 YARD CURL FROM BIG SPLIT	12 YARD CHOICE	FLAT	
3) IN	14 YARD IN CUT FROM BIG SPLIT	5 YARD UNDER	10 YARD IN CUT	

This simplicity is one of the reasons coaches around the league have been gravitating to the Erhardt-Perkins approach. "Concepts benefit you because you can plug different guys into different formations, into different personnel groups, and if they understand the concept, it gives you more flexibility," Tampa Bay offensive coordinator Dirk Koetter has explained. "The number system restricts you because it doesn't allow you to cover all the combinations you want to use, so you have to get into so many tags that eventually you're calling everybody's route. In route concepts, one word can describe anything. In my experience, most kids can visualize one-word concepts better."

There have been some noted successes of the Erhardt-Perkins approach but it's had some failures, too, particularly the plight of Rich Kotite's Jets while Erhardt served as offensive coordinator. Ray Perkins, who hired Parcells while head coach of the Giants and was later head coach of the University of Alabama and Tampa Bay Buccaneers, was at Jones County Junior College in Ellisville, Mississippi in 2013 and now volunteers with a high school football team. The ideas underlying the system are sound, but it's the Patriots who have made it their own.

• • •

For many years, the Erhardt-Perkins offense was known as the original ground-and-pound, a conservative run-first offense summed up by Erhardt's mantra, "You throw to score and run to win."

With the help of his assistants, Belichick's primary innovation was to go from an Erhardt-Perkins offense to an Erhardt-Perkins system, built on its method of organizing and naming plays. The offense itself would be philosophically neutral. This is how, using the terminology and framework of what was once thought to be the league's least progressive offensive system, Brady and Belichick built one of the most consistently dynamic and explosive offenses in NFL history. From conservative to spread to blistering no-huddle, the tactics—and players—have changed, but the underlying approach has not.

Let's look at a play that has long been a staple of the Patriots' attack. This is actually two different concepts put together— "Ghost/Tosser"—which has the Patriots run the Ghost concept to one side and the Tosser concept to the other. Ghost has the outermost receiver, whoever it is, run a vertical route, one inside receiver run to a depth of roughly eight yards before breaking flat to the outside, and the innermost receiver run immediately to the flat. It's a form of the "stick" or "turn" concepts that essentially every NFL team uses. On the other side, Tosser means that the receivers run the double-slant concept. The diagram below is from the Patriots' playbook.

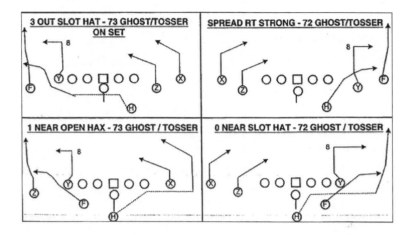

The theory is that no matter the formation, there is an outside receiver, an inside receiver, and a middle receiver, and each will be responsible for running the designated route. For the quarterback, this means the play can be run repeatedly, from different formations and with different personnel, all while his read stays effectively the same. Once receivers understand each concept, they only have to know at which position they're lined up. The personnel and formation might cause the defense to respond differently, but for New England those changes only affect which side Brady prefers or which receiver he expects to be open. This conceptual approach is how the Patriots are able to run the same basic plays, whether spreading the field with four or five receivers or using multiple tight ends and running backs.

The most recent innovation to fall into New England's Erhardt-Perkins framework is a commitment to the no-huddle. For example, in 2012, the Patriots were the league leaders in total plays, first downs, points, and yards—all by significant margins. Other teams have dabbled in the no-huddle, but they can't commit to it like the Patriots can, for one simple reason: terminology. No team that uses traditional Coryell or true West Coast terminology can adapt easily to a fully functional up-tempo no-huddle, because they can't communicate that efficiently. The Patriots are built to communicate in one- or two-word designations, and so, with judicious use of code words, it's a matter of translating what they already do into a no-huddle pace.

This marriage of terminology and technique, of efficiency and elegance, is what makes the Patriots so mesmerizing. Like NFL offenses, in recent years NFL defenses have also become too wordy, relying on long-winded calls that designate scheme and technique and impractical checks. With the speed at which New England operates, the message for defenses has become clear: fix your terminology or perish. For opposing offenses, the mandate is less direct but just as imperative. The Patriots have set the standard for modern offense, and if teams are going to keep up, they'll need to change not how they play, but how they talk.

FIVE STORIES ABOUT THE SPREAD OFFENSE

1. NORTHWESTERN LEADS THE WAY

The modern shotgun spread offense was not born on November 4, 2000, when lowly Northwestern, coached by the late Randy Walker, defeated Michigan, but that was the day it no longer belonged to the fringe: It was the spread offense's coming out party. The 2000s was the decade of the spread offense in college football, and we're still feeling the reverberations of the tectonic shifts; what began in backwater practice fields, the synthesis of old ideas with new ones, is now omnipresent on most levels of football, with even the NFL adapting to these schemes in fits and starts.

Northwestern defeating Michigan at that time was unthinkable. But that Northwestern won 54–51—in regulation, without any overtime—over a Michigan team only three years removed from a national championship was truly shocking. Given those gaudy figures, probably the least surprising statistic was that Northwestern's quarterback, Zak Kustok, threw for 322 yards and four touchdowns in the win; that is pretty standard stuff for the quarterback in a spread offense in a victory. We'd seen big passing numbers from run-and-shoot quarterbacks, and Drew Brees, who played in a wide open offense at Purdue, routinely rang up big passing numbers on Big Ten opponents. Northwestern was a four-wide receiver, up-tempo, shotgun-spread team. Isn't the very purpose of that offense to put up big passing numbers?

But there was another statistic that day: Northwestern, with a 6.64 average yards per rushing attempt, racked up a staggering 322 yards. Three hundred twenty-two! That was the sort of number you only saw from wishbone or triple-option teams; not a four-wide-receiver shotgun team, and certainly not *Northwestern*.

Northwestern's running back Damien Anderson had 268 yards, but Kustok—hardly anyone's definition of a great athlete—added another 55 yards on the ground himself and was just enough of a threat on Northwestern's read-options to make Michigan respect him. And Michigan respected him enough that it made the rest of the game plan work. The key play for Northwestern that day was a basic read-option, invented by Rich Rodriguez at a small school named Glenville State. The offensive line blocked for an inside-zone running play—a blocking scheme Walker had used from a traditional formation just a few years earlier—while the quarterback watched the back side defensive end. If the defensive end either didn't move or came at the quarterback, Kustok handed the ball off to the running back. If the end crashed for the runner, however, Kustok kept it himself.

Read-options force defenses to approach offenses much differently. With traditional approaches, the quarterback knows

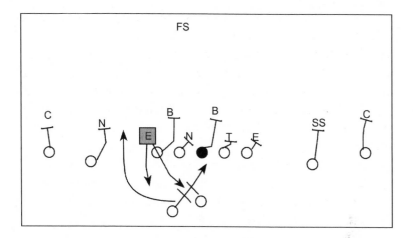

before the play whether he will hand the ball off or keep it. In a read-option, the quarterback, aligned in the shotgun, reads the movements of a particular defensive player, one the offense has specifically chosen not to block. It's based on this player's actions that the quarterback makes his decision—hence the (redundant) term "read-option."

The read-option thus forces defenses to bring in additional defenders to stop the run—but that's only the first step. According to Chicago Bears defensive coordinator Vic Fangio, on read-option plays offenses are "not even blocking one of the guys at the point of attack, so it actually becomes eleven against ten if they do it right. So, the numbers are flipped" (from a typical running play, in which the quarterback doesn't have to be accounted for). Read-option plays get a three-for-one. They add an additional offensive player whom defenses have to worry about, allow the offense to get additional blocks and double-teams by leaving a frontal defender unblocked, and allow the offense to block a defense's most fearsome defender with a player who has probably never blocked anyone in his life: the quarterback.

We're not where we are today because of the teams that spread the field with receivers running in every direction to throw. Instead, it was the promise of Randy Walker's Northwestern team and Rich Rodriguez's offenses at Tulane, Clemson, and West Virginia that there was a way to take on more talented opponents and *run the ball right down their throats*. As one high school coach put it to me at the time, "I don't want to throw it fifty times a game, and I don't have a Drew Brees on my team. But I do want to run the ball, and that Northwestern QB—slow, just-OK arm, but pretty good decisions—reminds me of my guy."

2. THE BIRTH OF THE QUARTERBACK

The 1940 Chicago Bears had one of the most dominating stretches of football in NFL history. Going into the final two weeks of the season, the Bears were 6–3 and had just lost 7–3 to the Washington Redskins. George Halas, Chicago's coach as well as its owner, decided the time was right for a switch in his offensive scheme. For help he turned to his good friend Clark Shaughnessy, the head coach at Stanford.

At the time, every NFL team ran the single wing offense, which featured a quarterback in the shotgun, an unbalanced line, and a direct snap to the tailback. But Shaughnessy used a different approach—first at the University of Chicago, where he and Halas became friends, and later at Stanford—by reviving the old T-formation, which placed a quarterback directly behind the center.

Shaughnessy's T-formation offense featured a variety of motions and misdirection to open up the running game, and he created an all-new passing attack, featuring the quarterback in ways that hadn't been done before. This combination made the offense nearly unstoppable—at least in college. Even as late as 1940, most pro coaches viewed the T-formation and its reliance on a quarterback taking the snap from the center, making fakes, and dropping back to pass as basically a gimmick. That is, until Halas's Chicago team adopted the T.

A week after losing to Washington, Chicago scored forty-seven points in a win over the Cleveland Browns and followed that up with another thirty-one in a win over the Chicago Cardinals. That set up a rematch: Chicago against Washington. Suffice it to say this one went a little differently, as quarterback (and future Hall of Famer) Sid Luckman led the Bears to a staggering 73–0 win to win the NFL title. And the last seventy years of NFL history have revolved around prototypical, T-formation quarterbacks.

Although few changes in football are as revolutionary as Halas and Shaughnessy's T-formation offense, most still tend to take the same route to acceptance: they begin on the fringe, the doodlings of some offbeat coach who probably never won anything, until some breakthrough moment when suddenly it seems like every team is using some version of the idea.

3. NICK SABAN'S HYBRID SOLUTION

Under Nick Saban, Alabama is known for running a 3–4 defense—meaning three defensive linemen and four linebackers. But that common description doesn't quite describe the practical reality on the field. "We are a 3–4 defense. That does not mean we play the 3–4 all the time," Alabama defensive coordinator Kirby Smart explained at a coaching clinic. "Last year [2013], we ran the 3–4 front 25 percent of the time. The rest of the time we played 4–3."

The reason for the shift is that offenses have been changing, so Saban and Smart's Alabama defense has changed with them.

Saban's 3–4 was designed as a run-stuffing defense for traditional attacks, but teams like Texas A&M are far more likely to spread the field. "When we play a two-back team, we are in a 3–4 defense. Georgia and LSU are two-back offenses," said Smart. "If a team is a one-back offense with three or four wide receivers in the set, we match their personnel and play nickel or dime. When we play nickel or dime, we play very little 3–4 defense out of it; we are in the 4–3 front."

And when facing one of these spread attacks, Saban likes to adjust his pass coverages as well. As he explained a few years ago, "When you're playing a passing team, you always have a better chance with split safeties," meaning coverages with two deep safeties. Against spread offenses, the blueprint has thus been straightforward: four down linemen, two deep safeties, and corners rolled up on the outside receivers. With this mixture, Saban's defenses have suffocated team after team: the attacking four-man line pressuring the quarterback, the cornerbacks rolled up to take away the quick screens, and a two-deep safety look from which Alabama can mix and match coverages to confuse the quarterback.

This approach works well if a team majors in either running or passing, as Saban can adjust his defense accordingly. Issues arise, however, if an offense is balanced, and can make his two-deep safety defenses pay with the run. If that's the case, then the defensive philosophy shifts. "Sometimes you've got to be able to play middle-of-the-field coverage to get an extra guy in the box," Saban said. In other words, "You have to have some guts and play press."

But what if the running team can also throw? Saban has answers for this, too.

• • •

In 1994, the Cleveland Browns under head coach Bill Belichick went 11–5 during the season, and tacked on an additional win in the playoffs over the Patriots. But they lost three times that season to the Pittsburgh Steelers, including in the divisional round of the playoffs. Belichick and Saban, his defensive coordinator at the time could not stop Pittsburgh's offense, especially from one-back sets. "Pittsburgh would run 'Seattle' on us, four streaks. Then they would run two streaks and two out routes, which I call the 'pole' route, from two-by-two," recalled Saban during a lecture to coaches. "Because we could not defend this, we could not play three-deep [zone], so when you can't play three-deep zone, what do you do next? We'll play Cover 1 [man-to-man coverage]. But here's the problem with Cover 1: If their men are better than your men, you can't play Cover 1, because they've got someone you can't match up with."

This was a concern, but had Pittsburgh purely been a throwing team, it wouldn't have been much of one. The Steelers were not, however, purely a passing team. In 1994, the Steelers led the NFL in rushing, something Belichick and Saban were brutally aware of. "So now we can't run Cover 1, and these guys can run the ball," Saban said. "We lost to [the Steelers] three times. And you know why? We could not play eight-man fronts against them to stop the run, because they would wear us out throwing it."

The question was how to find a way to get an extra defender in the box without playing a true, pure mano-a-mano defense. As Saban put it, "How can we play Cover 1 and Cover 3 at the same time so we can do both and one would complement the other?"

Had the coaches not been named Saban and Belichick, it's likely that the Steelers beating the Browns three times in 1995 would have been the end of the story. But instead, those two coaches devised a new tactic called "Rip/Liz Match," though neither got to put it to much use in Cleveland. Saban left to coach Michigan State, and Belichick was fired from Cleveland after failing to make the playoffs. But each has used Rip/Liz Match on his subsequent championship teams.

Rip/Liz Match is a pattern-matching adjustment to a traditional three-deep zone, which means that the zone defenders essentially play man-to-man coverage after the receivers have run the called pass pattern. Below is an image from Saban's playbook on Rip/Liz:

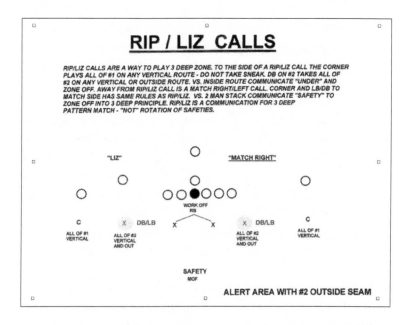

The insight behind Rip/Liz is that when offenses—like the Steelers in 1994—want to defeat three-deep zone, they run the tight end and slot receivers down the seams, but if they want to defeat Cover 1 man, they run picks and crossing routes. In response, the safeties and linebackers read the movements of the slot receivers and tight-ends. When those inside receivers run vertical, the nickel defenders and linebackers run vertical with them, but if those receivers instead quickly break outside or inside, those linebackers and nickelbacks, rather than chasing the receivers across the field, become zone defenders and drop into coverage.

"If [the receivers] run vertical, it looks like Cover 1 man coverage," Smart said in 2013. "It is unless the receivers start to cross; then it becomes zone. We play zone until the offense tries to run four vertical receivers down the field." And the most important benefit is the defense can now add an extra defender to the box to stop the run—or spy the quarterback.

• • •

Right now, at every level of football, defensive coaches have been racking their brains, trying to find a way to stop the onslaught of deadly dual-threat quarterbacks, particularly those captaining up-tempo spread attacks. Twenty-five years ago, Saban and Belichick developed Rip/Liz in order to match numbers against one-back offenses that could both throw and run. The fact that both coaches remain at the top of their games is strong evidence this tactic still works.

4. THE READ-OPTION, THE PISTOL, AND THE NFL

Around five years ago, Greg Roman, then offensive coordinator at Stanford University (and now the offensive coordinator in Buffalo by way of the San Francisco 49ers), traveled to Reno, Nevada, to visit with Nevada Wolf Pack head coach Chris Ault to learn about his "Pistol Offense." Before the 2005 season, Ault, unhappy with his offense, presented his staff with a new idea: a shotgun formation with the running back aligned directly behind the quarterback. "They thought I'd lost my marbles," Ault said at a coaching clinic in 2011. But with the pistol, Nevada went from near the bottom to the top of its conference in offensive production.

The potency of Ault's offense peaked during the 2009 season when they finished the season with three 1,000-yard rushers—two running backs as well the Wolfpack's lanky junior quarterback, a Colin Kaepernick, who added another 2,000 passing yards and 20 touchdowns. The following offseason, Roman, along with many other coaches from across the country, visited Ault. He wanted to learn how to add some pistol looks to the pro-style offense he ran at Stanford under head coach Jim Harbaugh. During their visit, Ault was, according to Roman, "very accommodating, and it was very interesting as a coach to go really learn something totally new," he said.

"There are no gimmicks in our offense," Ault has explained. "When the shotgun offenses came out, I enjoyed watching those teams move the football. The thing I did not like was the idea of a running back getting the ball running east and west," he said. "We have always been a north-and-south running-game offense."

The entire premise of Ault's pistol attack is to combine the best of the shotgun-spread offenses with the traditional, north-south power attack Ault had coached for more than twenty years. The pistol alignment–a shotgun formation with the running back aligned directly behind the QB–is merely the means by which to do it; Ault's Pistol Offense is this blend of old and new.

It is easy to see why Ault's vision had more appeal to the NFL mind-set more than the east-west schemes of other spread offense gurus. The NFL is a league concerned with its image, and despite the efficacy of those spread offenses, for the NFL to adopt something as its own it must appeal both to the ego and the mind. And when the read-option—an umbrella term for shotgun plays where the QB is reading a defender to decide whether to hand off or run—finally made it to the NFL it was Ault's pistol that was the means.

• • •

When Ault, now retired from coaching, installed his offense, he would begin with the same basic downhill inside-zone running play that every NFL team uses. (Zone blocking is a method for determining whom the offensive line will block one-on-one, who will be double-team, and which linemen will block linebackers.) Inside zone is essentially a straight-ahead play. Initially, at least, there are no reads for the quarterback to make—he just makes a hand-off. Typically, when Ault called the inside zone with no quarterback read, he called for "slice," a term that tells the fullback or tight end to seal the back side defensive end, a block that will, hopefully, create a cutback lane for the ball carrier. That is football 101.

Then it gets interesting. After slice, Ault installed "bluff"—another scheme NFL teams are now using. Bluff is Ault's take on the zone-read. The quarterback and running back turn away from where the base-run play is going so the quarterback can read the defensive end to the back side, who is not blocked, to determine whether to hand the ball off or keep it himself. The running back also begins away from the side the play is going. His job is to open his arms and take the hand-off only if the quarterback decides to give it to him, and then bend his path to the play side.

The other element to bluff is the "arc" block. The fullback or tight end loops around the defensive end—making it look the same as slice—but instead of sealing him off, the blocker bypasses him to take on the first defender in the alley, typically an outside linebacker. Not only is this effective deception, it is also designed to defeat most common defensive responses to the zone-read, as it provides a personal protector for the QB if the defense sends an extra safety or linebacker to hit the QB.

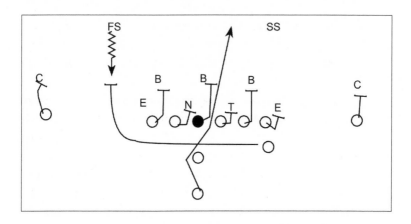

• • •

There was never any doubt pistol and read-option concepts would eventually be adopted by NFL coaches, not necessarily as the core of an offense but as a tool within a larger arsenal. "As I've tried to explain to people, whenever the guy who takes the snap is a threat to run, it changes all the math of defenses," former Rutgers and Tampa Bay Buccaneers head coach Greg Schiano said in 2013. "That's really what defense is. It's getting your troops to where the ball is going to be. And when that guy holding it is a threat to run, it changes the numbers: minus one."

And as Nick Saban learned long ago, the math problem isn't just an issue for stopping the run. The other reason, maybe the major reason, the NFL has cautiously embraced the read-option is that they now see the effect these schemes can have on passing. When the quarterback is a threat to run, defenses must stack the line of scrimmage, opening up passing lanes and one-on-one matchups for wide receivers outside. "You do read-option, read-option, read-option and then get them to play seven or eight in the box, and then you've got variations of plays and passes you can run off that," Carolina Panthers quarterback Cam Newton has said.

Aside from Chip Kelly's Philadelphia Eagles, no NFL team has embraced the read-option more than Pete Carroll's Seattle Seahawks, in large part because of the unique talents of their QB, Russell Wilson. "It opens you up to the possibility of things to do," Carroll explained. "It was a good move for me, and [the read-option] has helped us. I was influenced a little bit more than I thought when I first looked at it. You see some of our stuff coming to life."

5. SCRAPE EXCHANGES AND BEYOND

When the read-option first became prevalent in college football, defenses tried to defend it the same way they defended traditional run plays. "The defense fit defenders into every gap to the run side of the zone play," zone-read inventor Rich Rodriguez explained at a coaching clinic in 2013. "The back side defenders ran as fast as they could to the ball and watched for the cutback." In other words, the defense cared only about the running back and largely ignored the quarterback. The only job of the defensive players away from the run's initial path was to stop the running back from escaping out the back side. "That has all changed," Rodriguez said. "Defenses fit the front side of the defense one way and fit the back side another way, because the quarterback is a threat to run the ball."

Now, defenses use a variety of tactics against read-option plays. The most popular changeup is the "scrape" or "gap exchange," in which the back side defensive end and linebacker swap responsibilities—the end crashes for the running back while the linebacker scrapes for the quarterback. When the quarterback sees the end crash, his read is to pull the ball and keep it, a choice that will result in him running directly into a waiting linebacker.

That second player doesn't even have to be a linebacker. Under Saban, Alabama constantly varies the defender assigned to the quarterback. When Saban or Kirby Smart gives a "force" call, that tells a secondary player he is executing a gap exchange with the defensive end. "The quarterback sees the crashing end and pulls the ball," Smart says. "We roll the free safety down to the line of scrimmage, and he has the quarterback." And all this varies based on the opponent. "If the quarterback is a better runner, we make him give it to the tailback," said Smart. "If the tailback is the better runner, we give the force call, and the defensive end crashes inside and makes the quarterback pull the ball."

Not all the problems with defending are tactical. Back side defenders—usually the very players the quarterback is reading—have an especially difficult job. "The defensive end gets the shaft because he has to play two aspects: the dive, and the bend of the dive to the inside out to the QB," said Dave Aranda, Wisconsin's defensive coordinator. This is also why the old just-hit-the-quarterback tactic is not optimal, at least as an every-down strategy. If the defensive end or linebacker gets upfield too quickly, that means he is not squeezing the cutback and may be opening up a huge lane for the quarterback.

And what about defending Chris Ault's bluff tactic, where a tight end arc blocks as the QB's personal protector? "The Will [weak side] linebacker widens with that [arc] block," explained Mark Stoops, former Florida State defensive coordinator and current Kentucky head coach. "The defensive end squeezes to the dive back. If the quarterback pulls the ball, the defensive end pursues inside to outside. The Will linebacker squeezes the arc and forces the ball back into the end. He wants to condense the space. The free safety cheats down, fills the alley, and helps the Will linebacker play the quarterback." To stop the zone-bluff arc—a play that combines the finesse of the college read-option with the power-based blocking the NFL adores—defenses must use tactics and personnel that combine speed with strength.

• • •

So long as the battles are on notepads and whiteboards instead of on the field, both offensive and defensive coaches can claim the upper hand. But there are trade-offs on both sides. "There is," according to Stoops, "a weakness to every call we make." The goal is to hide and vary the weaknesses.

For defenses, the issues are requiring safeties and other typically pass-first defenders to spend so much time focused on the running game, leaving them vulnerable to the pass. The trade-offs for offenses are no less tricky, however. "The problem is for those quarterbacks. One of these days, one of them is not going to get up and walk off," said longtime NFL defensive coordinator Gunther Cunningham. "It's a lot of pressure on him to physically do that."

Given the premium on (and scarcity of) quality passers in the NFL, the read-option won't ever be the complete centerpiece for an offense, but that doesn't mean it's a gimmick, either. Gimmicks are plays that only work because they trick the defense; read-option plays instead do exactly what they are supposed to do: make a defender wrong every time, either by getting him out of position or blocking him with the reading player, the QB. Think of read-options like bootlegs, screen passes, draws, and other constraint plays that work by taking advantage of defenders who cheat and get out of position. One doesn't call a read-option because one *wants* the QB to keep the ball, but instead the read-option is called because it forces the defense to play honest, thus opening up the rest of the offense.

THE QUARTERBACK CURVE

Jim Mora's "Playoffs?! Playoffs?!" rant is, along with other feel-good moments like "They are who we thought they were!" and "Go play intramurals, brother!" in the pantheon of unhinged postgame outbursts. Resurrected every year just prior to, yes, the playoffs, it sticks with us because in one nasal-inflected word, Mora revealed everything about himself at that moment: he was a doomed man, something confirmed just weeks later when he was fired.

Yet the most interesting aspect of the rant is that almost everyone forgets the real target of the coach's ire. Mora was squarely and publicly laying the blame for his team's ugly loss to the 49ers at the feet of his team's young franchise quarterback—some guy named Peyton Manning.

"Do not blame that game on the defense, OK?" said Mora. "When you turn the ball over five times—four interceptions, one for a touchdown, three others in field position to set up touchdowns—you ain't going to beat anybody."

Keep in mind that, by 2001, Manning had been to the Pro Bowl twice and had compiled a 23–9 record over the prior two seasons. Still, Mora was unrelenting. "I don't know who the hell we think we are when we do something like that," said Mora. "Unbelievable. Pitiful. It's absolutely pitiful to perform like that." Although publicly ripping your franchise player is hardly advisable, Mora wasn't wrong; Manning had played poorly, and his twenty-three interceptions that season—coupled with the league's thirty-first-ranked scoring defense—had gone a long way in sending the Colts to a 6–10 record, ultimately costing Mora his job.

Few remember that Mora was talking about Peyton Manning because Peyton Manning has spent the last fifteen years making us forget. Manning has been so good for so long that we can barely remember a time before he and his chief rival, Tom Brady, were the game's best. Mora's tirade acts as a reminder that not even Manning arrived in the NFL as a fully formed star quarterback. He and Brady had their own struggles early on; the remarkable thing is not the heights they reached but how far they had to go to get there.

Since Mora's outburst, Manning has become a Super Bowl champion and solidified his status as one of the greatest quarterbacks of all time. He's closer to the end of his career than the beginning, and before long, he and Brady will be off to sell pizzas or pick Kentucky Derby winners or do whatever else football immortals do when their playing days are over. When they do move on, the spots atop the quarterback hierarchy will be open again, and the question will be who takes up the mantle. Aaron Rodgers looks like a lock for greatness, but the other contenders—Russell Wilson, Andrew Luck, and Joe Flacco, among others—are by no means finished products. Each has a long way to go before he can be considered a master of his craft.

No position is more scrutinized—How tall is he? How far can he throw? Who is he dating?—and nowhere in football is greatness valued or debated more, but exactly how young, promising quarterbacks become Tom Brady and Peyton Manning remains something of a mystery. The results are apparent, but most are unversed in the actual process. Manning, Brady, and Rodgers are great because they've taken the raw materials of the position—an understanding of defenses, of why receivers get open and how to find them—and transformed them into muscle memory they can use to fluidly perform every time. Greatness isn't something quarterbacks stumble upon. It's something that becomes ingrained into their very constitution.

• • •

It's no secret Peyton Manning works pretty hard. In April 2013, he and his brother, Eli, along with their top pass-catching targets, spent time on Duke's campus with Blue Devils head coach David Cutcliffe, who coached Peyton and Eli in college. At this stage, both brothers have seen their share of football but in traveling to Durham, Peyton wanted to go back to the beginning. He asked Cutcliffe for a return to the basics, to "coach us like we were both freshmen at Tennessee or Ole Miss."

When Cutcliffe trains young quarterbacks, he begins with their most valuable asset: their minds. "I do not talk about passing routes with them for one month," Cutcliffe said at a coaching clinic in 2011. "All we do is teach them defense for a month. We teach them the history of defense. We teach them the history of the zone blitz. We teach them what it is, and what is happening in the defense. Once the quarterbacks learn coverages, it enables them to move on in the teaching progression."

In football's earliest days, the forward pass was primarily about surprising the defense or attacking a single, isolated defender locked in man coverage. As defenses got more sophisticated, offenses evolved too, with the largest contribution coming from former San Diego Chargers head coach Sid Gillman, the "father of the passing game." Gillman refined passing into a calibrated, organized attack. His insights inform every throw you'll see on Saturdays and Sundays.

Realizing that a football field is nothing more than a 53⅓-yard-wide geometric plane, Gillman designed his pass patterns to stretch defenses past their breaking points. His favorite method was to divide the field into five passing lanes and then allocate five receivers horizontally in each one. Against most zones, at least one receiver would be open. Below is an image from one of Gillman's final playbooks with the Philadelphia Eagles.

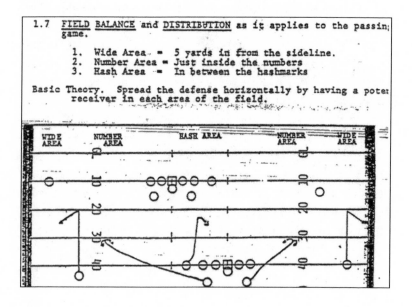

Along with stretching defenses left to right and right to left, Gillman also stretched them deep to short, by putting two or three receivers on the same vertical line. With Gillman's ideas in mind, well-designed pass plays today still combine horizontal or vertical stretches, with routes also designed to defeat man coverage. This means that as long as a quarterback can read the defense, he can find an open receiver. That, however, is the trick. As Gillman liked to write in his quarterbacks' playbooks, "You must know the theory of all coverages. Without this knowledge, you are dead."

A quarterback translates his knowledge of defenses and passing plays to the field through his reads, of which there are two basic types: progression and coverage. "A progression read is a pass play where three or more receivers are looked to in a one, two, three progression. 'Is he open? Is he open? Is he open?'" said Cutcliffe. With a coverage read, it's "the coverage played by the defense" that determines which receivers the quarterback looks for.

A few decades ago, basic if-then coverage reads were the most common way to teach a young quarterback how to find an open receiver. If the key defender dropped one way, the quarterback threw the ball to, say, his tight end, but if the defender dropped the other way, the quarterback threw it to the wide receiver. As defenses have become increasingly sophisticated, quarterbacks now need more options than simple key-defender reads provide. The answer was the progression read, which forces a quarterback to look at one receiver after another until he gets to the first open man. The progression read removes the need to look directly at defenders, but it doesn't mean a quarterback should be looking directly at receivers, either.

"I don't tell our guys to look at a defender," Georgia head coach Mark Richt has explained. "If our quarterback is looking at a defender, then his vision is too tight. Let's say he looks at the Will [weak side] linebacker, and the Will linebacker flies out to the flat. If he flies out to the flat, I better hit the slant, right? Well, what if the Mike [middle linebacker] runs that way and picks your slant? It's because you told him to look at the Will."

The quarterback isn't looking for defenders. He's instead looking for passing lanes—open windows through which he can throw the ball. "I tell them to look to the area," said Richt. "You look to the slant area, to the curl area. If there's nothing between you and him, throw it in there. If there's someone in the throwing lane, then go to the next read."

Most modern passing plays may use progression reads, but that still leaves open the question of which progression, and the answer is what brings everything together. It's a coverage read that determines the quarterback's progression. It was Gillman who developed one of the earliest and most effective tools for this, the idea of the "best-located safety," which he defined as the "safety that is lined up in a position that is least likely to be able to assist in the coverage of a wide receiver. In other words, he's the farthest removed and best to attack!" Most NFL teams still use the idea of the best-located safety as a coverage key, but it's only one of several.

Good passing teams package different pass concepts together to give their quarterbacks answers versus a variety of defenses. The coverage read on a given play is tied to these pass concepts. For example, if the route combination to one side is better against single-safety defenses like Cover 3, and the concept to the other side is better against two-deep, split-safety coverages, then the quarterback's read will be based on the number of safeties.

Given the byzantine schemes defenses have used in recent years, simple coverage keys aren't always enough to identify an open receiver. Aside from the usual veteran quarterback tricks— look-offs, dummy signals, and so on—Brady and Manning are better than other quarterbacks because they can process more information. They see not only the number of deep safeties, but the depth and leverage of the cornerbacks and the alignment of the linebackers. They see the entire defensive structure.

This is not to say they always (or even usually) know the exact coverage, but their years of study and practice allow them to make an instant judgment about the basic tactics of a defense—and where it's weakest. For example, while mounting a furious comeback against the 49ers in 2013, the Patriots lined up with a different route concept to each side of the formation: a curl/flat concept to Brady's left and the Levels concept to his right. Curl/flat is a horizontal stretch on the defense that works best against single-safety defenses like Cover 3, whereas Levels is a vertical or high/low stretch that works best against two-safety defenses. New England tied those concepts together with a seam-read route by Wes Welker, whose job was to either stay up the seam against a single middle safety or split two deep ones.

Brady's progressions on this play were (1) seam read, (2) curl, and (3) flat; or, if looking the other way, (1) seam read, (2) deep square-in, and (3) short square-in. What made his task more difficult is that the 49ers typically use a lot of hybrid defenses, frequently playing different coverages to each side of the field, specifically to confuse a quarterback's coverage keys. Brady looked off the safety, saw that Welker was not open on the seam read, hitched up in the pocket as he refixed his eyes to the receiver running a curl, and delivered the ball to the curl for a first down.

• • •

No matter how much he's prepared, for an NFL quarterback, the moment just after the snap is mayhem. Cornerbacks who looked like they were in soft coverage before the snap roll up to press receivers, unexpected blitzers come tearing off the edge, and savvy safeties start on one side of the field, only to fly to the other. It's also the most critical moment. Regardless of what bizarre look the defense shows before the snap, once the play begins, it must reveal its true intentions.

This is why, on their initial steps away from the line—the first step in a three-step drop, or the first three steps in a five-step drop—quarterbacks must keep their eyes directly down the middle of the field and use their peripheral vision to see how the defense, in particular the safeties, rotate and align. Gillman called this "reading the square," and not only is it crucial for a quarterback's read, it also provides a natural look-off. The quarterback gives nothing away when he looks deep down the middle. By the end of his drop, the quarterback should grasp enough of his coverage read to decide which progression of receivers he'll look to. At that point it's as simple as reading one, two, three—in theory.

The next step is not only making the right read but making it at the right time. Receivers in the NFL are open for only the briefest of moments, and according to Bill Walsh, "Too often either the quarterback is standing there waiting for the receiver, or the receiver has broken before the quarterback can throw the ball." In the NFL, being too early or too late is just as fatal as being wrong.

Careful calibration of the timing between quarterbacks and receivers is a fundamental element of making an offense work. By defining a quarterback's drops by the specific number of steps taken, offenses can synchronize the quarterback's movements with the routes of the receivers; the timing between when a quarterback is ready to throw and when the receiver is ready to receive the ball must be perfect. Specifically, the quarterback's first read should be thrown to when his last step hits the ground. This is what is known as a "rhythm" throw.

Now, let's say the quarterback's first read isn't open. How does he know when to move to the next receiver? The idea of finding a secondary receiver leaves some quarterbacks looking like they just lost their wallet. For others, like Brady or Manning, it looks easy, and it's because it's not only their brains telling them when to look.

"His feet are telling him when to move to number two and number three," Michigan head coach Jim Harbaugh said to a room full of quarterback coaches back when he was coaching at the University of San Diego. "One-two-three-four-five-plant— throw it. If it's not there, first hitch is to the [second read], and then the second hitch is to the [third read]." This must be precise. "If you have a passing system where he's dropping back and waiting for a guy to come open, a lot of bad stuff is going to happen," said Harbaugh.

...

Often we associate being great with being spectacular, but that's the secret about playing quarterback: great quarterbacks seek the banality of perfection. It's about avoiding the bad play, hitting the right receiver, making the right read, and throwing an accurate pass every time. Mora's outburst is infamous, but he was absolutely right when he said you cannot win if your quarterback makes critical mistakes.

The process of becoming that player is only so complex. Defenses, reads, and coverages can all be learned in time. It just takes a truly dedicated player with a disciplined mind to see that process to its end. Played out as far as it will go, those decisions and movements are no longer conscious ones. For the best quarterbacks, it goes beyond making the right read and correct progression. The elements of great quarterbacking become a part of their very makeup as players. According to Bill Walsh, "Because of the dynamic role he plays on the team, a quarterback must have physical, mental, emotional, and instinctive traits that go well beyond the mere ability to pass a football." If the league's young quarterbacks want to be truly great, they'll have to master something that comes from the combination of all those traits, something that can't really be coached, something Brady and Manning have both done for years.

"Does he make everyone around him better?" said Cutcliffe in 2011. "We have all played with those types of quarterbacks, we have coached them, or we have seen them. That is the greatest gift the quarterback can have."

TOTAL PACKAGE: "PACKAGED PLAYS" ARE CHANGING HOW WE THINK ABOUT OFFENSE

"Those things usually happen at happy hour."
– *West Virginia head coach Dana Holgorsen,*
on inspirations for tactical innovations

With the opening game to start the 2012 season against Southern Cal just weeks away, then Syracuse head coach Doug Marrone had a serious problem: his offense. Marrone, who would later become head coach of the Buffalo Bills, seemingly had all the pieces needed to be successful. Marrone followed his tenure as a highly respected NFL offensive-line coach with three seasons as offensive coordinator for one of the league's most prolific offenses, the Drew Brees-led New Orleans Saints. At Syracuse, he had a quarterback considered a possible early round pick, Ryan Nassib, and had been recruiting his own players for several seasons. Yet in 2011, Syracuse finished ninetieth in total offense, as they transformed a somewhat promising start into a disappointing 5–7 record, including five straight losses to end the year.

Marrone and his offensive coordinator at Syracuse, Nathaniel Hackett, son of longtime NFL coach Paul Hackett, spent the offseason trying to figure out how they could fix a pro-style offense that was supposed to take college football by storm. The answer was to go the other direction—to learn from the top college offenses. Marrone and his staff spent extensive time that summer studying teams like Oregon, Clemson, and West Virginia to figure out how to blend their up-tempo, spread-it-out philosophies with the NFL concepts Marrone and Hackett believed in. And after the first couple weeks of training camp showed little improvement on the prior year's results, Marrone called for the switch that would change the course of his career.

"Two weeks before the season, we changed the whole offense," Hackett explained after Syracuse's 2012 season. And the theme for all the changes could be summed up in one word: compression. It wasn't that Marrone added a bunch of new plays, or that the changes were obvious enough that a casual fan would notice, but the entire framework of the offense was changed. For the passing game, Marrone said his first priority was to reduce the number of passing concepts. Out too went the complicated NFL-style play calls, replaced with simple, one- or two-word commands that facilitated the team's new up-tempo, no-huddle pace.

What was most interesting, though, was how Marrone and Hackett began compressing plays together, combining multiple concepts into a single play and then letting Nassib figure out on the fly whether to, say, throw a quick pass, throw a screen, hand off, or keep the ball himself—all on the same play.

The result was that in 2012 Syracuse set its all-time record for total offense, went 8–5, won its bowl game, and finished 6–1 down the stretch as the players settled into the new offense. Nassib was drafted by the New York Giants, and Marrone and Hackett wound back coaching in the NFL, with promotions. Not bad for keeping it simple.

• • •

Combination or "packaged" plays have been sweeping across college and high school football over recent years, enough that NFL coaches are clearly taking notice. These plays, which are sometimes also called "run/pass options," combine running and passing concepts into a single play, meaning that the offensive line might block for a run play while receivers run pass routes or screens, and it's up to the quarterback to decide whether to hand off or throw it out wide.

Good offense has always been about deceptive simplicity. The clearest path to success is to make things as simple as possible for your players while also keeping defenses off-balance. It's a difficult recipe, as an offense that is too simple can get dissected, analyzed, and shut down by a savvy defense, but a team that tries to do too many things will master none of them. Packaged plays solve the quandary by combining simple plays anyone can execute in such a way that—if the quarterback makes the right decision—the offense always has the advantage, because no defender can be in two places at once.

Consider a series from Ole Miss's bowl game against Pittsburgh at the end of head coach Hugh Freeze's first season in 2012. Until recently, Freeze was probably most famous as the high school coach from the book and movie *The Blind Side*, but with his team's surprising success, he's beginning to earn a reputation as an innovator. The official play-by-play description for the touchdown drive looks a lot like the description for any number of similarly successful drives:

- Play 1: eight-yard rush
- Play 2: completion to a receiver for four yards, first down
- Play 3: quarterback run for thirteen yards
- Play 4: completion to a different receiver for five yards
- Play 5: completion for eighteen yards, touchdown

That description seemingly represented what everyone watching the game saw—Ole Miss kept Pittsburgh's defense off-balance with a mix of plays that resulted in a quick, efficient scoring drive. Except that wasn't the case at all. Ole Miss did not choose five different plays to keep the defense confused. Instead, five times in a row they ran the same play – a play that had four different options all built in.

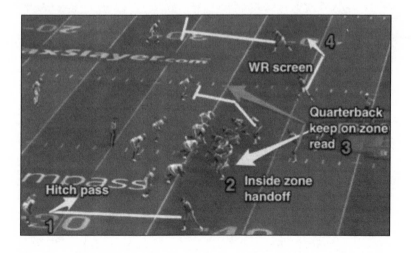

Ole Miss combined a five-yard hitch route to the single receiver to the left, an inside zone, a quarterback read-option keep, and a receiver screen to the offense's right. And as a final wrinkle, their tight end ran an arc release to block an outside linebacker.

The quarterback's job was to first determine if the defense had enough defenders near the line to stop the run. If not, he read the read-option play, handing it off or keeping it himself. If the defense did have enough defenders inside, he either threw the screen pass or the quick hitch to his left. Ole Miss combined a very simple play concept with an extremely fast version of the no-huddle, and while it is the defense that dictated whether the statisticians counted it as a run or pass, the offense got what it wanted: a touchdown.

That little drive in a semi-meaningless bowl game represented a potent shift in how coaches think about play calling in the modern age, and a video game will help illustrate why.

• • •

Still maddeningly addictive, the old Tecmo Bowl video game had an extremely basic but intuitive play-calling system. Each team had four plays to choose from on offense—usually two passes and two runs. There were also four choices on defense, but rather than choosing from the set of sophisticated coverages, blitzes, and fronts available in today's football games, players instead chose what play they thought the *offense* would run. If the guess was correct, the offense's failure was preordained: the quarterback would be sacked or the runner tackled for no gain. If wrong, two of the options might only go for a moderate gain, but the third meant catastrophe for the defense.

Admittedly or not, most fans think of real-world play calling as a slightly more complicated version of the Tecmo Bowl model. The offense's job is to keep the defense guessing, and the defense must guess right to make a stop. On some level, even with their lengthy play sheets and reams of data, professional coordinators are engaged in a version of this same psychological battle, employing little more than educated guesses about the opponent's tactics. Until recently, even the best, from Bill Walsh to Bill Belichick, have been playing what amounts to a complex game of Tecmo Bowl, improved only by the marginal differences coming in the form of various checks or audibles by the quarterbacks.

That little drive by Ole Miss reveals that things are no longer so straightforward. There's a new game, and it takes those time-tested plays and blends them into something new. And it blends them so seamlessly that it threatens to upend the very ideas of run and pass. The answer to "What play was that?" is increasingly, "All of them."

It's understandable that most fans (and even many coaches) think of football plays in terms of the strict run-pass dichotomy of the Tecmo Bowl model. Fantasy football is founded on the difference between passing and rushing statistics, and even recent scholarly articles about football are built upon the distinction because that's what shows up in the box score. And at least on some level, the idea of packaging multiple options for the quarterback based on the movements of defenders is not entirely new. But the trend of combining entirely different categories of plays—runs and passes, screens and passes, runs and screens—is new, and these ideas are at the forefront of thinking about football.

"The basic premise is to make a key defender be in two places at the same time," said Keith Grabowski, a former college offensive coordinator. "We're only scratching the surface of what's possible."

One of the most interesting packaged concepts—and the play that first helped me begin to rethink the very nature of a football play—is known as "stick-draw," which combines a delayed run, or draw play, with the quick-passing stick concept. The first coach I saw put it in action was Dana Holgorsen, the current head coach at West Virginia. Like all of the best packaged concepts, nothing about the play is particularly new. It's the elegance of assembly that is important.

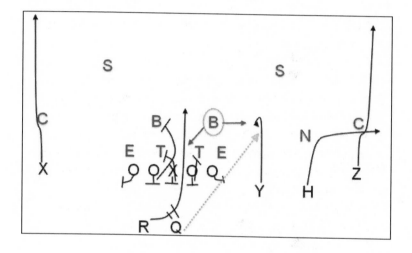

These combination plays are designed to focus on a particular defensive player, referred to as the "key" defender. In the case of the stick-draw play, it's a linebacker, who stands as an unchecked threat to stop the draw and the quick inside-pass route. The traditional answer was to have the QB call an audible, but the problem with that is even savvy QBs can be fooled with pre-snap tactics. The better answer is to build the play itself around the key defender, and to read him. Enter packaged plays.

As the offensive line and running back execute the running play, and the wide receivers execute another, it's up to the quarterback to decide. Here, he's the one hitting the Tecmo Bowl button, but it's done after the play has begun so he's no longer guessing: The defender has committed, and the right play is obvious. If the key linebacker flies out for a pass route, the quarterback hands the ball to his running back; if he steps up for the run, the QB fires the ball to the receiver for a quick, ball-control pass.

"It's a run/pass concept. We will count the numbers in the box," North Carolina assistant coach Seth Littrell said of a similar packaged play. "If they give us the numbers in the box, we will run the ball; if they load the box up, we will throw a slant to the open space." (Linemen are actually allowed leeway in getting downfield on pass plays, and in college they have up to three years. In the NFL, they can be a full yard downfield when the ball is thrown. As Littrell says, they tell the linemen "to block the run scheme that's called, and we'll get the ball off quick enough to where linemen aren't downfield.")

It's no surprise then that packaged plays have swept across football. Cal offensive coordinator Tony Franklin began packaging downfield pass routes with run plays after seeing Holgorsen give a lecture on the concept at one of the seminars Franklin runs for high school coaches. "I went to my seminar the next year and said to Dana, 'Please, let's keep this within our family. Don't tell anybody. Maybe we can get five years out of it,'" Franklin told CBSSports. "In 2012, maybe five to ten college teams were doing it with full-route concepts. Now it's half of college football doing it. We got two good years out of it."

• • •

The beauty of these plays—and the reason they have been rapidly adopted, not just in college football but also in the NFL—is that while they use the QB as a decision-maker to help the run game, they do it without putting him at risk. In short, packaged plays are read-option football for quarterbacks who can't run the read-option. And they are particularly devastating when combined with that other rampant trend in football, the up-tempo no-huddle. "In the no-huddle context, the advantage of packaged plays becomes particularly acute," said Grabowski. "An offense that can run these packaged plays at the fastest tempos can get a vanilla look that further simplifies the read on a key defender." If you're going to go fast-paced no-huddle to prevent defenses from substituting or setting up in something exotic, you have to do it, well, fast, and slow audibles with lots of words and gyrations at the line are not that.

The Tecmo Bowl model has been the dominant model since long before Tecmo Bowl, but this new approach is an opportunity to take the old trusted tactics and adapt them for the modern game. And, as Grabowski points out, we've only just begun. "The only limit to packaging plays seems to be a coach's creativity in finding different ways to make a single defender wrong, every time."

SMU head coach Chad Morris, one of the most innovative coaches in the NCAA, had a slightly different answer when asked about packaged plays. "We run the triple option," said Morris. "We just don't run it the way they used to run it."

A DEFENSE TO MATCH

Mark Dantonio and Pat Narduzzi shared a sideline for more than a decade, first at Cincinnati and then at Michigan State, and in the process they forged one of college football's great coaching pairings. In recent years, Dantonio, Michigan State's head coach, and Narduzzi, MSU's former defensive coordinator and now the head coach at Pittsburgh, together won a Big Ten title, returned the Spartans to the promised land of Pasadena, and accomplished something even more exceedingly rare: In the age of the wide-open offense, they built a shutdown college defense.

Along with defending champion Florida State, Michigan State was the only team to rank in the top five in defensive yards per play in each of the 2011, 2012, and 2013 seasons, and the Spartans finished number one in 2013 in that category while posting a 13–1 record. And in 2014, the Spartans posted an 11-2 record and finished with the top rushing defense in the country. Even more remarkably, Dantonio and Narduzzi have built one of the best defenses in the sport without the benefit of the kind of blue-chip, future-NFL talent that's commonplace at schools like FSU, LSU, and Alabama. Instead, they've done it with great teaching, an emphasis on fundamentals and technique, and a uniquely simple yet adaptable defensive scheme.

. . .

The paradox of the offensive explosion that's swept college football in recent years is that, particularly when coupled with the no-huddle, offenses have actually enjoyed more success by getting simpler. Five-hundred-page playbooks have given way to play-call sheets the size of Post-it Notes, and given the NCAA-mandated limits on practice time, the mantra has been that fewer plays rehearsed more often will defeat just about anything a defense can think up—so long as the quarterback makes the right read.

Just by lining up, modern spread offenses pose three threats on essentially every play. First, each of a team's multiple receivers is a threat to streak straight downfield in the form of four verticals, which puts tremendous strain on the defense by outnumbering traditional two-deep and three-deep zones. Second, those receivers can also crisscross and run underneath pick routes, which makes life difficult for defenders trying to play man-to-man coverage. And third, particularly if the quarterback is a threat to run, these offenses can still rush the ball. Defenses have individual answers to each of those tactics, but as the increased level of scoring around the country proves, defending all three at once is a tall order.

Rather than trying to call the right defense and maybe being right or maybe being wrong, Dantonio and Narduzzi responded to this challenge by building a responsive defense that mutates into the right alignment, depending on what the offense does. Against four vertical receivers, Michigan State wants four man-to-man defenders who can carry the receivers all the way upfield; against crisscrossing underneath receivers, the Spartans want to be in a zone coverage that lets their defenders break hard on the ball and on those receivers, rather than forcing them to chase in man-to-man; and against the run, the Spartans want as many as nine defenders in the box.

How do they manage all that at once? Down after down, Michigan State lines up in what looks like the same basic, predictable front, with apparently the same coverage behind it: a 4–3 Over front paired with "Quarters," which is also known as Cover 4. (Like Dantonio and Narduzzi, I use those two terms interchangeably.) The 4–3 Over is the oldest and most straightforward front in football, and it's exactly what fans think of when they hear "4–3," as it features four defensive linemen and three linebackers behind them. Quarters or Cover 4 coverage is a little trickier. While it's a zone coverage, it doesn't merely call for four defenders to drop to a deep zone, as the name might seem to imply. It's played with considerably more nuance, particularly at Michigan State.

At a 2009 coaching clinic, Dantonio described Quarters as "tight man in a zone coverage with good run support that self-adjusts to various formations and routes." The key part is "self-adjusts to various formations and routes," because MSU's Quarters isn't so much a single coverage or defense as it is a set of principles that allows the Spartans to handle just about anything an offense tries.

MSU's scheme depends on the safeties, who have to make the most adjustments. They begin much closer to the line than most teams' safeties, usually around eight or nine yards deep, and numbering the offense's eligible receivers from the outside in, they look through the number-two receiver to the offensive line for their initial keys. If the number-two receiver runs past that eightish yard mark, he belongs to the safety in what's essentially man-to-man coverage. But if that receiver runs a short route inside or outside, the safety passes him off to the linebackers helping underneath and becomes a "robber" player, keying the number-one receiver and the quarterback while trying to intercept any throws to the inside.

If it's a run play, however, the safeties join the four defensive linemen and three linebackers in stuffing the run. "Why Cover 4? We get nine men in the box," Narduzzi said of his defense. "People talk about, 'Man, we're in an eight-man front.' Well, we're in a nine-man front." Getting that safety help against the run gives Michigan State's linebackers flexibility rarely seen in other systems and allows them to follow one overarching rule: see ball, get ball. There's a reason the Spartans' rushing defense has ranked in the top ten nationally every season since 2011.

Unlike most teams that use Quarters coverage, though, Michigan State challenges receivers by putting its cornerbacks in tight press coverage, in part for philosophical reasons. "Our front is an attacking front, and the press corner fits the mentality of the defense," explained Narduzzi in 2011. The other reason is more practical. Eschewing conventional wisdom, Dantonio and Narduzzi sincerely believe it's easier to play press coverage on the wide receiver than to play off of him. Against press, a receiver has fewer routes he can run and must declare right away which ones he's running as he releases inside or outside at the snap. Against soft coverage, however, a receiver has the freedom to run any route he wants without giving clues to the defense. Thus, it actually "takes a better player to play off the receiver than in press coverage," Dantonio said at the clinic. "If the corner can run and has good balance, he will be a better press player than an off-player."

Just because it looks like man and smells like man, however, doesn't mean it's actually man coverage, a mistake offenses frequently make. "Some guys might say, 'That looks like man coverage. You're manned up,'" said Narduzzi. "We're not manned up. It's zone coverage."

Because it's zone, the Spartans' cornerbacks benefit from inside help from linebackers and safeties, and if the number-one receiver runs a short route, the corner will typically let him go and drop into a deep zone.* A pass coverage that's at once zone and man-to-man is hard for opposing QBs to decipher.

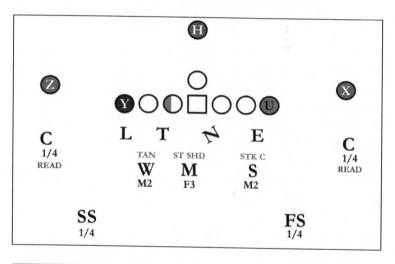

---

* To be technical, Michigan State gives its corner either a "Meg" or a "Mod" call, depending on the game plan and situation. Meg, the more common call, tells the cornerback to drop into zone if the receiver breaks off his route short. "Mod," or "man on demand," tells the corner to instead play the receiver in man coverage no matter what he does. Against formations with three receivers to one side, the cornerback on the back side is given a call of "Yo Yo," which stands for "You're On Your Own."

Of course, many defenses that look great on paper have failed on the field, and for Michigan State's adaptable Quarters scheme to succeed, every defender needs to make the same reads. And that's precisely why the Spartans don't run myriad defenses, instead preferring to master one highly sophisticated, flexible approach.

"I believe one defense can stop everything; I believe we could play an entire football game in our base defense," explained Narduzzi. "I believe that if everyone lines up exactly right, reads their keys, and does all the fundamentals involved with the defense, it is enough to win."

. . .

All defenses need changeups, though, even those as good as Michigan State's. The Spartans' most potent alternate look has been their package of blitzes, which, like the rest of what they do on defense, is simple and adaptable. "We like zone pressure over man pressure," said Narduzzi. "The main—and only—reason is [zone blitzes] are safe and easy." In contrast, he said, "In man pressure, if you miss a tackle, it's all the way to the house, and the band is striking up, and we are getting ready for kickoff." Narduzzi's not kidding, as he noted that in 2010, Michigan State blitzed 31 percent of the time, or 276 times total, yet ran only seven man-to-man blitzes to 269 zone blitzes. And while Narduzzi and Dantonio frequently give clinics describing their Quarters coverage, they're decidedly more tight-lipped when it comes to blitzing specifics. "We're more cutting edge [with] zone pressure," Narduzzi told ESPN in 2014. "We do a lot of things people don't do, and to be honest, people are trying to copycat it all over the country."

For years, the zone blitzes Dantonio and Narduzzi ran were the traditional fire-zone blitzes that every team used, with five blitzers and six defenders in coverage arranged as three deep and three underneath. But in the last few years, Michigan State has heavily featured a tactic few other teams employ: a six-man blitz with five defenders in zone coverage. All-out, "Cover 0" man-to-man blitzes are used at every level, but they're very risky, and Michigan State likes its blitzes safe. The answer, three deep-zone defenders with two underneath, has overwhelmed opponents in recent years.

The most famous six-man blitz Michigan State uses is the old "double-A" gap blitz, which sends two linebackers right up the middle on either side of the center. Even that, however, has an MSU twist: Dantonio and Narduzzi arrange their six rushers in a wide variety of ways, looping defensive tackles, crashing ends, and using linebackers and safeties off the edge. Playing only five defenders in pass coverage is meager, however, and the reason most teams play straight man-to-man behind a six-man rush is to account for all the eligible receivers.

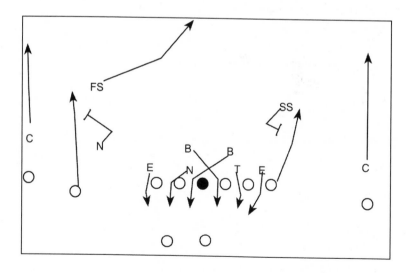

Michigan State solves this issue by having the two underneath defenders look to initially take away any "hot" or in-breaking routes that come into the seam area and then read the quarterback's eyes. The key is not to have perfect pass coverage, but to have pass coverage that's adequate enough while the quarterback is under extreme duress. By its own calculation, Michigan State blitzes on only around 30 percent of its defensive snaps, but because those blitzes are well-timed and well disguised, they often leave the biggest wounds.

• • •

Dantonio and Narduzzi know that great D isn't the function of a magical scheme; it's about mastering fundamentals and playing with discipline and effort. The scheme is there merely to channel the players' energy and help them play fast and without hesitation. Right now, no defense in college football does that better than Michigan State's.

THE INFLUENCER: CHIP KELLY

"**M**y high school coach was a prototypical old football coach," former Oregon and current Philadelphia Eagles coach Chip Kelly said during a packed coaching clinic lecture in 2009. His coach at Manchester Central High School in New Hampshire was Bob Leonard, and he was definitely old-school. "We ran an unbalanced, two-tight end, power-I formation," Kelly said. "We averaged five passes a game." When Kelly joined Leonard's staff after he finished college, he tried bringing with him a few of the principles he'd learned while at New Hampshire. "I told him that in college we split players [out wide] and threw the ball to them. He thought that was a bunch of college bull."

Eventually, the future spread offense maven broke the old coach down. During one practice, a receiver left the huddle— they huddled back then—and trotted out toward the sideline. Not a single defensive player followed. "The defense thought he was going to get a drink," said Kelly. Convinced he'd seen a glimpse of the future, Kelly excitedly pointed out the uncovered receiver. The old coach turned to the younger one and said, "Good. Now get him back in the box so he can block somebody."

...

Since Kelly became Oregon's offensive coordinator in 2007 and its head coach in 2009, the Ducks have rolled up incredible statistics to go along with a fantastic won/loss record, even after he departed for the NFL in 2013. And in his first season as head coach in Philadelphia, Kelly's team led the NFL in rushing, rushing yards per carry, and explosive plays, they were second in total offense, and the Eagles posted back-to-back 10–6 records after going 4–12 in 2012 prior to Kelly's arrival. The most common explanation for this success is Kelly's up-tempo, no-huddle approach and the theory that simply running plays quickly is what transforms a good offense into a great one. There's an element of truth to this—the no-huddle is undeniably key to the identity of Kelly's teams both at Oregon and in Philadelphia—but the explanation is incomplete. Kelly doesn't use his fastest tempo all the time, and the benefits of the no-huddle go well beyond those sixty electrifying minutes on Saturdays and Sundays.

Kelly's anecdote about his old high school team suggests another possibility. Chip Kelly's methods work not because they are gimmicks, but instead because rather than choose sides between old and new, Kelly's teams straddle history. Kelly has been successful because his teams have done well what good teams have always done well, albeit with a little more flash, a little more science, and a slightly more modern wardrobe.

OREGON DUCKS: WIN THE DAY

"Every coach has to ask himself the same question: 'What do you want to be?'" Kelly said at a lecture for high school coaches. "That is the great thing about football. You can be anything you want. You can be a spread team, I-formation team, power team, Wing-T team, option team, or wishbone team. You can be anything you want, but you have to define it." Kelly's choice of a no-huddle spread offense still drips from every corner of the impressive practice facilities in Eugene, and Oregon does not run a no-huddle offense so much as they are a no-huddle program.

And for all of the hype surrounding Oregon games, Oregon practices might be even better. Oregon practices are filled with blaring music and players sprinting from drill to drill. Coaches interact with players primarily through whistles, air horns, and semi-communicative grunts. Operating under the constraint of NCAA-imposed practice time limits, Oregon's practice sessions, which still track the Kelly model, are designed around one thing: maximizing time. For Kelly, the practice field is for repetitions, while traditional coaching—correcting mistakes, showing a player how to step one way or another, or lecturing on this or that football topic—is better served in the film room.

The up-tempo, no-huddle offense ends up benefiting in practice as much as it does in games. Without time wasted huddling, players get many more practice repetitions, leading to increased efficiency on Saturdays. As Sam Snead once said, "Practice is putting brains in your muscles," and Oregon's up-tempo practices are all about making Kelly's system second nature.

When the games do begin, there's no question that the no-huddle makes Oregon's attack more dangerous, but it's a common misconception that they have only one supersonic speed. The Ducks use plenty of their superfast tempo, but they actually have three settings: red light (slow, quarterback looks to sideline for guidance while the coach can signal in a new play), yellow light (medium speed, quarterback calls the play and can make his own audibles at the line, including various check-with-me plays), and green light (superfast).

This change of pace is actually how Oregon constantly keeps defenses off balance. If they only went one pace the entire game, the offense would actually be easier to defend. When the defense lines up quickly and is set, Kelly takes his time and picks the perfect play. When the defense is desperate to substitute or identify Oregon's formation, the Ducks sprint to the line and rip off two, three, or four plays in a row—and it rarely takes more than that for them to score.

While the coach-player interaction may be limited during Kelly's practices, it's significant before and after them. At its most fundamental, Kelly's system is a carefully organized, carefully practiced method for forcing defenses to defend the whole field and then exploiting those areas left exposed. And the first tool Kelly uses is a surprising one: math.

• • •

"We spread the defense so they will declare their defensive look for the offensive linemen," Kelly has explained. "The more offensive personnel we put in the box, the more defenders the defense will put in there, and it becomes a cluttered mess." Twenty years ago, Kelly's high school coach ran the unbalanced, two-tight end power-I so he could execute old-school, fundamental football and run the ball down his opponent's throat. Today, Kelly spreads the defense and operates out of an up-tempo no-huddle so he can do the exact same thing.

"If there are two high safeties [i.e., players responsible for deep pass defense], mathematically there can only be five defenders in the box. With one high safety, there can be six in the box. If there is no high safety, there can be seven in the box," Kelly explained. The easiest case is if the defense plays with two deep defenders: "With two high safeties, we should run the ball most of the time. We have five blockers, and they have five defenders."

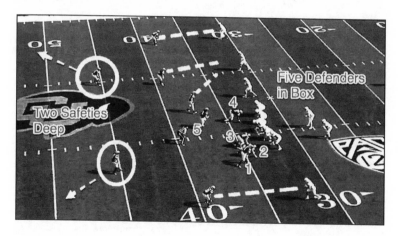

As Penn State's excellent offensive line coach, Herb Hand, told me, "I tell my offensive line that if the defense plays two safeties deep, it's like spitting in your face—it's a lack of respect for your run game." Oregon's run game doesn't suffer from any lack of respect; as a result, they rarely face two-deep defenses except on obvious passing downs.

When a team brings that extra defender into the box, the calculus for the offense changes. "If the defense has one high safety and six defenders in the box, the quarterback has to be involved in the play," Kelly explained. "He has to read one of the defenders, in effect blocking him. We can block five defenders and read the sixth one."

Most teams facing Kelly's Oregon teams played with a single safety deep in an effort to have a sufficient number of defensive players to stop Oregon's vaunted rushing attack, but Kelly and Oregon had answers. For example, in the 2012 Rose Bowl against Wisconsin, De'Anthony Thomas ripped off a 91-yard touchdown run that left a very good Wisconsin defense in the dust. Yet Thomas's blazing speed might have been the least interesting element of the play.

Most modern defenses employ "gap control," meaning that they assign a defender the responsibility to fill a certain space between offensive linemen. If the defense successfully fills this space, they will "spill" a runner to the outside—right into oncoming defenders. By alignment, Wisconsin had all of the gaps covered. The problem was that because Oregon had two backs in the backfield—Thomas and Kenjon Barner—the defense needed an additional defender to account for the gap a lead blocker can create when a runner goes to either side of him. By walking a safety down into the box, Wisconsin had accounted for this too. Against a traditional offense, the Badgers' defense was sound.

But one of the areas where Kelly is a master is in messing with a defense's efforts at gap control. Coaches have long used a variety of methods to manipulate a defense's keys and assignments, from using unbalanced sets to extra tight ends to lead-blocking fullbacks and pulling linemen who can remove and add gaps that must be defended. Kelly uses those tactics, too, and they're blended into a mix of deadly spread concepts and old-fashioned, excellent blocking.

On the play against Wisconsin, Kelly packaged an inside-zone running play with a "zone read triple option" to the back side. With the option, the quarterback's job is to read the back side linebacker. If the linebacker stays put, the quarterback hands it off to a running back. If the linebacker crashes toward the back, the quarterback keeps the ball and takes it outside. And if after keeping the ball the quarterback is threatened by another defender, he has the option to pitch the ball to another running back running behind him. The idea was to mess with that carefully calibrated gap-control defense and set up the thing Kelly really wants to do—the same thing his old high school coach wanted to do—run the ball right up the gut.

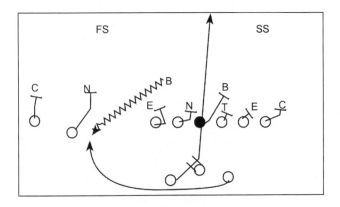

As a result of big plays like this, some defenses decided the best way to slow down Kelly's Ducks was by selling out to defend the run. Kelly has answers for this, too. As he has explained, "If there are seven defenders in the box, there are only four defenders to play the pass. It is difficult to play man-to-man without help all day long." The first thing Kelly does if a defense entirely loads the box for the run is to recall the lesson he (indirectly) learned from his old high school coach: make the defense cover the spread receivers by throwing them the ball.

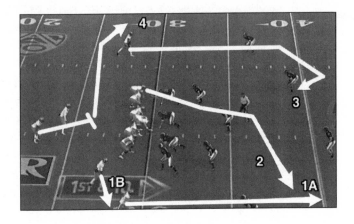

For example, Kelly's favorite pass play at Oregon was known as "Saints," which was simply their version of the old deep-cross concept that has been around for decades. Kelly always runs the play with play-action, with a running back faking an inside-zone or sweep play. While the QB fakes the ball to the running back he eyes his first reads, the receivers labeled "1A" and "1B," who are running a streak and a bubble route respectively. Which one the QB focuses on depends on how the defense is aligned, but generally the QB wants to peek at the bubble route underneath to draw up defenders but actually read the deeper streak route for a potential big play.

But if both are covered, the QB will reset his feet and look for the deep-crossing route, in this case the tight end, whose job is to read the drops of the linebackers and the safeties to determine whether to break flat across the field or drift farther upfield, wherever there is more open space. Indeed, the play is really designed to get the ball to the tight end on the crossing route, as the linebackers are likely to step up at the threat of the run. And if the cross isn't open, the QB will again reset his feet, this time looking for the back side receiver who is running a deep curl, and finally his check-down receiver is the running back in the opposite flat. To this day, Oregon runs this play several times in every game they play.

PHILADELPHIA EAGLES: WEIRD SCIENCE

When the Philadelphia Eagles hired Chip Kelly away from Oregon in January 2013, they thought they were getting a coach who'd field an innovative offense run at a madcap pace. What they probably didn't realize, and what the rest of the league surely didn't know, was that they were also getting a coach who intended to rethink much about how NFL teams operate, from huddling (why bother?), to traditional practices (too much wasted time), to player nutrition habits (bye-bye, Andy Reid's fast-food Fridays).

If they didn't realize this, they should have, because Kelly has always challenged the status quo—sometimes even to an uncomfortable degree. "I was probably a pain in the ass as a little kid," Kelly said recently. "I questioned everything. I've always been a why guy, trying to figure out why things happen and what they are and just curious about it from that standpoint."

The result of all of that questioning was a successful debut season for Kelly, whose Eagles went 10–6 and won the NFC East one year after going 4–12 under Reid. The NFL has a conflicted relationship with new concepts, as defiance often gives way to rapid-fire assimilation. And unsurprisingly, that's already happening with Kelly's ideas.

So far, most of the attention surrounding Kelly has centered on his spread offense, particularly the way in which he gives his quarterbacks multiple run, keep, or pass options on the same play, all from a no-huddle, up-tempo pace. And those ideas are certainly having an impact. The Dolphins hired Kelly's quarterbacks coach, Bill Lazor, to implement a version of Kelly's scheme in Miami; the league in general is trending toward more no-huddle; and several NFL coaches have told me their teams are now using "Chip Kelly plays."

But Kelly's influence extends far beyond read-options and the no-huddle, and into the subtler and more fundamental aspects of the game. Kelly's question-everything approach has caused many smart NFL coaches and executives to ask themselves why they've been doing things the same way for so long. And many are realizing that Kelly's answers are better.

•••

It's hard to get a first down in the NFL. The defenders are fast, the tactics are sophisticated, and the state-of-the-art technology and exhaustive scouting reports mean there are no secrets. What's innovative one week is passé the next. As a result, modern NFL game planning is an arms race of minutiae, with coaches sleeping on couches and sifting through hours of film in an effort to find even the smallest advantages.

Over the last twenty-five years, however, there have been increasingly diminishing returns on spending thirty-five hours a week engineering a situation in which there's a 41 percent chance that a receiver who runs a 4.43 forty will match up against a cornerback who runs a 4.47 on a seven-yard route. In the last few years, NFL offenses have begun changing drastically to find a better way, and Kelly's teams have been at the forefront of that evolution, first at Oregon and now in the NFL.

Now that Kelly's Eagles have found success, the conversation has shifted away from whether his offense would work in the NFL to whether that success is sustainable, and particularly whether defenses will have figured out the attack. This line of questioning misses the mark, however. Kelly's offense isn't unique because of specific schemes; it's unique because of how he organizes and implements them.

"I've said it since day one: We don't do anything revolutionary offensively," Kelly said in 2014. "We run inside zone, we run outside zone, we run a sweep play, we run a power play. We've got a five-step [passing] game, we've got a three-step game, we run some screens. We're not doing anything that's never been done before in football."

Instead of drawing up a new play to get that one-on-one matchup for that seven-yard pass, Kelly, like some football hacker, likes to attack the very logic of defenses by deploying two-on-one, three-on-two, and four-on-three advantages, whether in run-blocking schemes or pass patterns. This is why the Eagles led the NFL in plays of more than twenty yards in 2013. Kelly is actually trying to break defenses.

Take, for example, Philadelphia's 2013 season opener. Before the game, Washington defensive coordinator Jim Haslett said he'd watched not only the Eagles' preseason games, but also "twenty-three, twenty-four Oregon films." He thought he'd seen it all. He hadn't.

Early in the game, Kelly identified a particular weakness for Washington: an inability to properly defend Philly's "unbalanced" offensive-line sets. Kelly frequently puts Eagles offensive tackles Jason Peters and Lane Johnson to the same side while keeping only the offensive guard and a tight end on the other.[†] And in that week 1 contest, which the Eagles won 33–27, the Redskins repeatedly failed to account for interior gaps when the Eagles went unbalanced. In the play shown in the diagram, LeSean McCoy rumbled for a thirty-four-yard touchdown run, but it was clearly going to be a big play for the Eagles because Washington totally failed to account for a gap in response to Philadelphia's unbalanced line.

[†] Technically, because a tight end was back side, the formations were "tackle over" sets, not "unbalanced." But "unbalanced" is the common term.

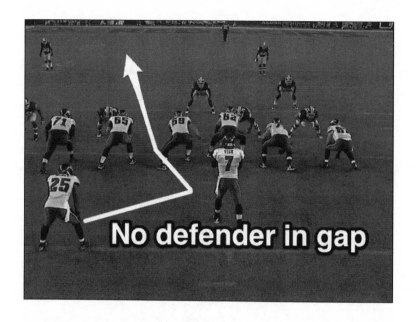

No defender in gap

Few of Kelly's opponents have fared much better against the Eagles' unbalanced sets, as he continually devises new iterations, particularly to his sweep play. Kelly's sweep is an updated version of a football classic: the old Green Bay Packers Vince Lombardi sweep, but with a particular wrinkle—a pulling center who leads the way for the runner. The best example of Kelly's take on the Lombardi sweep came against Lombardi's old team.

In the play shown below, explained Kelly, "We're in two tight ends on this [left] side, so there's concerns from a passing standpoint, but we have two tackles to the other side. With two tight ends to the left, the secondary support is on that side, so there's no secondary [run] support to [the right] side." In other words, because defenses try to match the strength of an offense's formation, Green Bay's safeties followed the tight end and wide

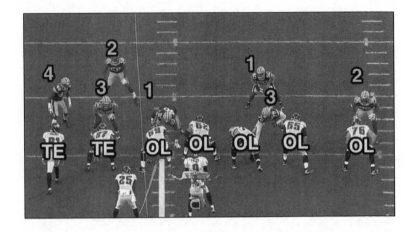

receiver left, which gave the Eagles a numbers advantage to the right: four blockers to handle just three defenders.

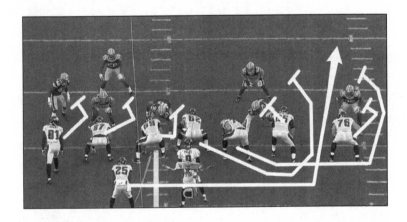

The result was another big run for McCoy—this time thirty yards, though it could have been much more—but the breakdown occurred not because Packers defensive coordinator Dom Capers doesn't know how to match up against an unbalanced set. (He does. I think.) It happened because against Kelly's offense, it often doesn't matter what the other coaches know. The eleven defenders on the field need to be able to identify the unbalanced set and call the right adjustments, on the fly, at a superfast tempo, while worrying about fifty other things.

"Through our formations and adjustments, we want the defense to show us how they are adjusting and playing us. We may go unbalanced or use motion to make the defense adjust," Mark Helfrich, Kelly's offensive coordinator and successor at Oregon, said in 2013. "Early in a game we want to show things we saw on film and watch the defensive adjustments. Defenses do not have time to adjust too much when you push the tempo. What the quarterback sees is what he generally gets."

With Kelly, it's usually about more than what we see. What makes him so interesting is his ability to seamlessly mesh old-school tactics and NFL-style attention to detail with an approach that attacks the very structure of defenses. College football has produced a lot of innovation over the last ten years or so, but many of the great college innovators lack the attention to detail to succeed in the NFL. At the same time, the old ways are too ingrained in many NFL coaches for them to adapt to an evolving game. Kelly has always been at home blending the old and the new. That's where the NFL is going, but Kelly is already there.

• • •

Despite his reputation for both innovation and secrecy, Kelly is surprisingly open about his Xs and Os. He even participated in a series of videos for the Eagles' team website, in which he candidly explained specific plays and the strategies behind them. But there are two subjects he refuses to openly discuss: his no-huddle communication system and the particulars of how the Eagles use sports science.

The former makes sense: Why would Kelly give out his signals so that opponents could steal them? Kelly's secrecy over his team's sports performance and recovery methods, however, points to his belief in the powerful competitive advantage that sports science provides.

From top to bottom in the Eagles organization, the first rule of sports science seems to be "Don't talk about sports science." Despite the limited information at our disposal, however, here's what we know:

- While coaching at Oregon, Kelly began investing significantly in sports science, both by bringing in outside consultants and by developing in-house expertise and technology. He built principally on research first conducted for Australian-rules football.

- Many of those studies, which have since been expanded to cover a range of sports, used heart rate, GPS, accelerometers, and gyroscope monitors worn by players in practice to determine how to train for peak game-day performance and how to prevent injuries. These studies also tracked the movements that players made in games so teams could mold practices and training to what players did on an individualized and position-by-position basis, with particular focus on avoiding injuries and training for peak performance on game days.

- When Kelly arrived in Philadelphia, the Eagles invested huge sums into their sports-science infrastructure, and Kelly hired Shaun Huls, a sports-science coordinator who'd worked for the Naval Special Warfare Command for nearly five years, training SEALs and focusing on reducing the incidence of their noncombat injuries. (Huls is a protégé of Boyd Epley, who founded one of the first and most successful strength and conditioning programs in football at the University of Nebraska.)

- Kelly's team uses the latest wearable player-tracking technology, and his staff monitors the resulting data in real time to determine how players should train and when they become injury risks. "On an individual-ized basis we may back off," Kelly has said. "We may take [tight end] Brent Celek out of a team period on a Tuesday afternoon and just say, because of the scientific data we have on him, 'We may need to give Brent a little bit of a rest.' We monitor them very closely."

- At least so far, it's worked. In addition to their on-field success, the Eagles were also the least-injured team in the NFL in 2013 and the fifth least injured in 2014, according to *Football Outsiders*.

- Just as important, the players think it works. "What happened with our players is all of a sudden when we started to get to game day every week, they were like, 'Wow, I've never felt this good,'" said Kelly. "And I know every guy, to a man, in December—Todd Herremans, DeMeco Ryans, Trent Cole, guys who've been around a long time—said I've never felt this great in December."

Of course, other NFL teams have begun using sports science, and every NFL team can afford to buy the same equipment and hire the same Australian consultants to churn out similar data. But there's a difference between having the data and knowing what to do with it, and Kelly and his inner circle have years of experience analyzing performance information for football. This is why Kelly is so tight-lipped. He knows that, eventually, other teams will catch up. But he's not going to help them get there.

Kelly makes the most practical use of his research where players spend the vast majority of their time: in training and at practice. By this point, it's common knowledge that Eagles practices are the most unique in the league. Like Oregon's practices, they feature blaring music (the team kicked off the 2014 training camp by playing "Return of the Mack" over the loudspeakers) and weird contraptions and drills. When Kelly took over, many commentators, former players, and coaches wondered whether his frenzied practices and up-tempo style in games would wear down his own players, particularly the veterans. Kelly accounts for this in his practice design and real-time workload monitoring.

Yet Kelly's practices are also frenetic because he believes that's the best way for his players to learn. "When we teach, we implement it in the classroom. We talk about what we are putting in that day," he explained in 2011. "After that, we go to the practice field and do it. The practice field is not where we talk. It is where we do the skills. We want to keep the words there to a minimum. The words you do use must have meaning. [Players] do not want to hear you give a ten-minute clinic in the middle of the field."

Kelly's chief commitment isn't to running a no-huddle offense; his goal is for the Eagles, like Oregon, to be a no-huddle organization. For Kelly, the benefits extend far beyond the effect on opposing defenses. "One of the benefits we have from practice and the no-huddle offense, where every period is no-huddle, is our second and third [teams]—and I've gone back and charted this—get almost twice as many reps as other teams I've been at when you're sitting in the second or third spot," explained Eagles defensive coordinator Billy Davis, a longtime NFL veteran. That has a recruiting benefit when it comes to attracting backup players, which in turn helps the Eagles discover hidden gems. "If you're [second or third string], you want to be in our camp because you get more reps than anyone else," said Kelly. "Because of the reps we get in practice, our guys get a chance to develop a little more. You go to some teams, and the threes aren't getting many reps—they are losing time compared to our guys."

The Eagles are different in how they practice, and also in when they practice. On the day before games, Kelly's Eagles conduct a full-speed, up-tempo practice, rather than the leisurely walk-throughs run by essentially every other team in the league. "Through our research, through science, [we learned] that you need to get the body moving if you're going to be playing," Kelly explained. "We used the same formula at Oregon, and I spent a lot of time on how to go about it, how we think you should train, and it worked for us there, and it worked for us here."

Specifically, while at Oregon, Kelly visited with trainers of elite Olympic athletes, and those trainers balked at the idea of doing next to nothing physically taxing in the forty-eight hours prior to competing. Kelly switched his approach and began conducting full-speed practice the day before games, and the results speak for themselves.

No NFL team practices more efficiently than the Eagles, and it's these little details that accumulate to help Kelly achieve big advantages in the untapped peak performance arena. Doing anything that much better, especially something as fundamental as practice, will eventually spawn copycats. And sure enough, following the 2011 collective bargaining agreement, which puts significant limits on the number and length of organized practices, other teams have been forced to play catch-up to methods Kelly has been using for years.

...

Shortly after Kelly took the Eagles job, one Oregon staff member gave me his read on Kelly: "What people think Bill Belichick is like—thinks about football nonstop, all day, every day—is how Chip actually is. He's a bachelor and has no kids. Football is what he's about." Focusing on football so completely, and questioning everything about the game, can't be the most peaceful way to live. But that's how Kelly's wired. He once told a room full of high school coaches—who were eager to hear his wisdom on how to coach the spread offense and draw up cool plays—that it "bothers" him when he visits a high school practice and sees "the coaches standing around talking to one another or throwing the ball around" while the team is stretching. Kelly's sense of humor is well documented, but when it comes to football, he's all business.

He knows his business is never finished. "I give myself a 58.8 percent," Kelly said after the 2013 season, grading his first season as an NFL head coach. "That's winning ten games out of seventeen." And his 2014 team missed the playoffs despite a 10-6 record. Kelly knows that if his team stumbles, he'll quickly stop being "Chip Kelly, successful innovator" and become "Chip Kelly, latest college coach to fail in the NFL." And he knows there's always another question to ask, another long-accepted belief to challenge.

Regardless of what happens in Philadelphia, Kelly has already sparked change that will outlast whatever his tenure in Philadelphia winds up being. "Coaching is one thing and one thing only. It is creating an environment so the player has an opportunity to be successful," Kelly told those high school coaches. "That is your job as a coach. When you teach him to do that, get out of his way." In turning a 4–12 team into a division winner, Kelly also reminded a lot of his NFL peers of that lesson and then showed them some new ways to act on it. Now it's up to the rest of the league to catch up—and up to Kelly to stay one step ahead.

THE POP WARNER OFFENSE THAT CONFOUNDED SEAN PAYTON

During his Roger Goodell-mandated suspension in connection with the bountygate scandal, which lasted the entire 2013 season, New Orleans Saints head coach Sean Payton spent his time coaching his son's sixth-grade pee wee football team, the Liberty Christian Warriors, who eventually went to the league championship game. The Warriors lost just two games all season, but both of those losses came against the same team, the Springtown Orange Porcupines.

For those familiar with Sean Payton, it shouldn't be a surprise that he took this seriously (well, at least mostly seriously). After losing to the Porcupines 38–6 in the regular season, Payton enlisted the help of some rather noteworthy former NFL coaches to help devise a plan that could slow down Springtown Orange's single wing offense. It didn't work: Payton's Warriors lost 58–18.

After the game, a gracious Payton spoke to both teams. "We spent all week, we talked to Bill Parcells and Jon Gruden and asked them how to defend the single wing," said Payton. "You have no idea how much time we spent. You guys put fifty-eight points on the board."

The single wing is, in many ways, football's original formation. Although hard to imagine now, there was a time in the NFL when using a quarterback under center was considered a gimmick, and nearly every team used some version of the single wing and other direct-snap formations. All that changed after the Chicago Bears destroyed the Washington Redskins 73–0 in the 1940 NFL Championship Game using the T-formation. But the single wing has not completely died out from football.

In particular, youth football has seen a resurgence of this most old-school of old-school attacks, as the combination of misdirection and overwhelming power—and the lack of a need for a sophisticated passing game—makes perfect sense for a bunch of fifth- and sixth-graders. (Many pee wee football leagues are named after Glenn "Pop" Warner, the coach often credited with inventing the single wing.) Rob Adams, Springtown's coach and a former TCU offensive lineman, went to the single wing after failing to find success using more modern schemes. Adams runs a version of the single wing attack developed by a youth coach named Dave Cisar, though Adams's brand is also heavily influenced by what he learned while playing for the man he calls a "surrogate father," his college coach, Jim Wacker.

In the traditional single wing, a few elements are combined into an attack that dominated football for decades and forced defenses to evolve in ways that remain crucial today: (1) some form of direct or shotgun-style snap, instead of an under-center exchange; (2) an unbalanced line, with more blockers to one side than the other; (3) an emphasis on power plays that outnumber the defense at the point of attack; and (4) a bevy of shifts, ball fakes, crisscrossing players, and all manner of misdirection.

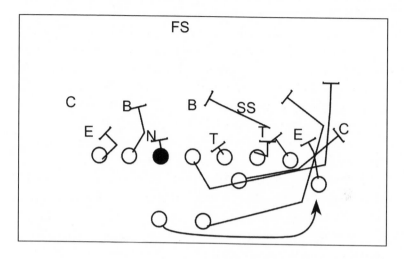

Adams's team has twelve plays, with names picked by his kids to help them remember their assignments: power is "pizza," spinner is "spaghetti," and so on. The important thing is not so much the plays but how they are taught and how they fit together. "We have a counter for every run and a fake off every counter," says Adams. Before going to this system, Adams says, he'd "never won anything [in football] at any level, including in college." But since taking over at Springtown Orange, he turned the team around in just a couple of seasons. If it's good enough to beat Sean Payton, with the assistance of Jon Gruden and Bill Parcells, does that mean Cisar, Adams, and others are onto something big?

Suggesting that, of course, seems absurd. Youth football and the NFL are obviously night-and-day different; it's laughable to suggest that because the single wing won a sixth-grade championship it could win a Lombardi Trophy, so laughable that no one would suggest it. No one, that is, except Vince Lombardi. "What would happen if someone came out with the single wing offense?" Lombardi once asked. "It would embarrass the hell out of us." And Lombardi wasn't alone. Roughly twenty years later, fellow Hall of Fame coach Bill Walsh said he'd "reflected on the single wing" and, in his view, "those blocking schemes would just chew up NFL defenses. You could double-team every hole and trap every hole."

Yet I think it's safe to say the single wing, at least the system as run by Adams, won't be the hot new (old?) thing in the NFL. Although many say that football is cyclical, that's actually only rarely true. Sure, some concepts or plays disappear for a while and then come back, but when they do, they're always adapted for modern times. The original versions vanished for a reason, often a defense's reaction.

But there is a kernel of wisdom here. There are many, many ways to be successful in football, and it wouldn't shock me at all to see elements of the single wing slowly find their way back into NFL offenses. Maybe we see more unbalanced sets, and an increasing use of misdirection seems likely as well. As much as any time in the past ten years, NFL coaches now seem willing to try all manner of new ideas. Maybe the single wing will be among them, maybe it won't. Maybe the fact that Payton, Gruden, and Parcells spent time thinking about how to stop a sixth-grade football team matters. Maybe it doesn't.

Until then, all we're left with is an experience a bunch of youth-football players will never, ever forget. "It was like fantasy camp for my players and coaches," said Adams of facing—and beating—a Super Bowl-winning coach. "And Coach Payton couldn't have been any more gracious to all of us, particularly the kids."

OLD MAN TRICKS

Peyton Manning entered the NFL with all the physical tools a team could want. He was six foot five and 230 pounds, with exceptional footwork and a natural throwing motion. But it's no secret he became one of the greatest quarterbacks of all time due to his work ethic and his otherworldly football aptitude. "[Manning]'s going to attack you based on what you're doing," Patriots coach Bill Belichick, Manning's oldest and most crafty adversary, said of him in 2013.

"If you do certain things, he's going to do certain things. If you do other things, he's going to do other things. He's going to run the plays that are good plays against what you're doing: runs, passes, screens, whatever they are. That's what makes him a great, great, great quarterback. He's very, very good at that."

Manning's most basic tools for extracting information from a defense are the snap count and his use of the no-huddle. "Sometimes they run up and snap the ball real quickly, so it forces you to get lined up," Belichick said. "Other times they go up there, and they delay and check the play and get into a formation that kind of makes you declare so they can see what you're in and then get to the play they want to get to and go at a very slow pace. It's hard to overdisguise, because if they go quick, then you could be way out of position."

Because he's in such control between plays, Manning has created a paradox: he often sees simpler and more basic looks than even the greenest rookie quarterback, which has allowed him to take a different approach from most NFL passers. For thirteen seasons with the Indianapolis Colts—spanning three head coaches, two Super Bowl appearances, one Super Bowl victory, four NFL MVP awards, and countless incredible games— Manning ran one of the simplest, most concise playbooks in the NFL, and he destroyed teams with it. And he did much the same thing after joining the Denver Broncos, following a serious neck injury that cost him an entire season, in large part by using the same plays he used in Indianapolis.

MANNING, MEET MOORE

Some years ago, when he was the offensive coordinator at the University of Florida, Larry Fedora went on vacation with his wife to Pawleys Island, South Carolina. Fedora, currently the head coach at North Carolina, ventured out to the golf course, and there on the practice tees he saw an aged, white-haired figure he thought he recognized. It was Tom Moore, then the Colts' offensive coordinator and something of a legend among the coaching cognoscenti. "I asked if he was going to play," Fedora recalled. "He was, and I asked him if I could ride the round with him." For an up-and-coming coach like Fedora, golfing with Moore—who not only was the man behind the record-breaking Colts offense but also a longtime NFL assistant, including during the Super Bowl years in Pittsburgh under Hall of Fame coach Chuck Noll—was like a scene out of

Almost Famous. Fedora was in heaven. "I rode eighteen holes with Tom Moore."

The two of them mostly talked about the kinds of things football coaches talk about away from the game, but the young coach worked up the courage to ask one real football question: When the chips are down, and you absolutely have to get a first down, what plays do you call? Moore's response was unexpected, in that he said there was only one choice. "He told me the play was so simple that I would not believe it," said Fedora. "He said it was Peyton Manning's favorite play."

The play Moore described *was* so simple that Fedora didn't believe it. But that play, along with a handful of others, helped the combination of Manning and Moore lead one of the most unprecedented runs in modern football history.

"I can give [you] the playbook," said former Manning back-up quarterback Jim Sorgi in 2010, Manning's last full season in Indianapolis. "There are not that many teams they're going to play who don't know what they're going to do. It's all about execution. Their coaches are like, 'We'll tell the other team what we're doing. They got to stop us.' That's what they do. That's what they're all about. And not many teams have been able to stop them yet."

Sorgi was not kidding. Outexecuting opponents is easier with number 18 and receivers like Marvin Harrison and Reggie Wayne, but the offense Moore developed for Manning drew strength from simplicity. By using a small number of personnel groups—typically either three wide receivers and a tight end, or two wide receivers and two tight ends—it limited the number of possible responses from the defense and made it easier for Manning to diagnose weak spots.

Combining just a few plays with just a few formations not only put the entire offense at Manning's disposal, it also reduced the number of tasks for players to practice which led to another Manning hallmark–ruthless precision. Despite media intimations to the contrary, the most sophisticated quarterback in the NFL ran what was arguably its simplest offense. It also just happened to be the best.

The play Tom Moore diagrammed on the back of a golf scorecard for Larry Fedora roughly a decade ago is a perfect example. Known as "Dig" in the old Colts playbook and as "Levels" to most coaches, the play has an inside receiver run a square-in or dig route while an outside receiver runs a five-yard, in-breaking route on the same side of the field. On the other side, an inside receiver runs a read-seam, either streaking up the seam if there is a single deep safety or breaking to the middle between two deep safeties. The image below is from Manning and Moore's old Colts playbook.

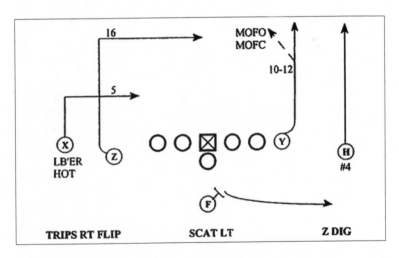

It's difficult to overstate how often Manning ran this with the Colts or how often he still runs it with the Broncos. Ten times a game in various forms and from different formations was not and is not uncommon, and in games in which he threw the ball a lot, the number was more like fifteen or twenty. Dig is Manning's Lombardi sweep: You know it's coming, but you can't stop it. Manning reads the play high to low: (1) the read-seam to (2) the deep dig to (3) the short in. He's been doing this so long that he can often directly zero in on where the ball needs to go.

But what made the Manning-Moore offense work was not merely having a finite number of plays; it was having a small number of plays that fit together. Too many NFL teams have plays for their own sake. The Manning-Moore offense had only what was necessary, including the first adjustment to Dig—the aptly named "Dag."

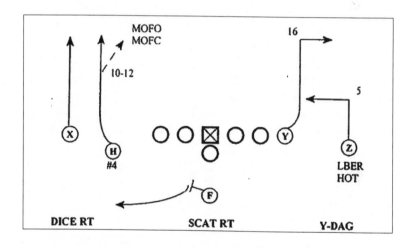

Dag is what most coaches call a "smash" or "China" concept, in which an inside receiver runs a corner or deep route over the top of an outside receiver who stays short. This creates a high-low read for the quarterback. The beauty of Dag is that to the defense, everything looks the exact same as Dig—right up until that inside receiver breaks outside, not inside.

ROCKY MOUNTAIN RISE

The Colts era is long over, and even the Manning-Broncos era appears on the downswing. But while Manning has yet to win a Super Bowl in Denver, he still put up incredible numbers and posted a 38–10 record in three seasons. But when Manning signed with the Broncos, the early wave of headlines—"Broncos' playbook will be new to Peyton Manning, not coaches" was an actual example—seemed designed to convince us that the Manning-Moore offense was gone for good.

As they gained exposure to their new quarterback, however, the stance of Denver's coaches slowly grew more flexible. Then Denver offensive coordinator Mike McCoy noted that he'd "be an idiot" not to listen to Manning; the goal how to find a "happy medium" between the approach of Denver head coach John Fox and what Manning had previously done.

And when Peyton Manning chose the Broncos, part of the decision came from him actually wanting to learn their schemes. McCoy had a well-deserved reputation for flexibility, a necessary trait given that his two quarterbacks prior to Manning were Kyle Orton and Tim Tebow. But when Denver stumbled out to a 2–3 start in Manning's first season there—and the team's offense was undergoing something of an identity crisis—the coaches and Manning realized something had to change. And the seeds for what that looked like were already there.

During that 2–3 start, the Broncos scored just under 70 percent of their points in the second half, often while trailing. It was during these stretches of urgency that, by necessity, Denver shed what was nonessential and went with what worked: a combination of what its players could do effectively and what Peyton Manning was comfortable with. Following their third loss of the season, the Broncos offense became what it likely should have been from the first day: as close to the Manning-Moore offense as possible. By the end of the 2013 season, the transformation was nearly complete, so when New England coach Bill Belichick was asked how similar the Broncos offense was to what Manning ran in Indianapolis, he was typically candid, saying, "It's identical. It looks the same to me."

...

Even though the actual plays in Manning's Denver playbook largely became the same ones he used in Indianapolis, the emphasis shifted. With the Colts, a large percentage of Manning's throws went to vertical-stem routes, where receivers ran straight down the field before breaking inside, outside, to the post, to the corner, or curling up. Those throws have been present in Denver—no one throws a prettier fade pass than Manning—but a big chunk of Manning's completions with Denver have been on plays designed to be thrown short. The goal on such plays is to throw short and let Denver's receivers run long, particularly with the "Drag" or shallow-cross series.

Denver ran the play diagramed here on the very first offensive snap of the game against New England in the 2013 AFC Championship game, resulting in a quick six-yard reception for Julius Thomas. Manning's Drag series has a set of rules for each receiver so that the play can be called from almost any formation. The play always begins by calling for a specific receiver to run the drag—i.e., Y Drag or Z Drag. From there, the other receivers' assignments fall into place. Specifically, the outside receiver to the opposite side of the drag runs a deep crossing route at a depth of eighteen to twenty yards (unless there's an additional rub signal, in which case he crosses at a depth of six

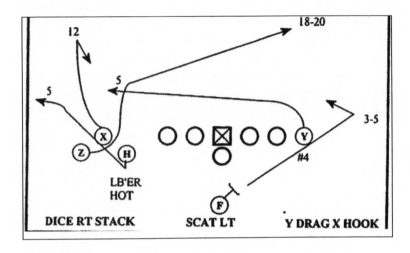

yards to create a legal pick play for the drag receiver); the running back runs an angle route or flat route and the other receivers run vertical routes, although typically at least one of them is tagged with a specific route, such as Z curl, Y post, and so on.

Manning's increased reliance on the Drag has been partially strategic, since it works well against the kind of press-man coverage many teams employ in lieu of letting Manning expose their zone coverage. It has also stemmed from physical concerns. Manning's arm strength, while still serviceable, is obviously not what it once was. But much as Michael Jordan shifted from slashing and dunking to employing a crafty and basically unstoppable fadeaway jumper as he aged, Manning has adapted to his physical limitations by relying on his anticipation, his ability to process defenses, and his knack for delivering accurate passes to receivers on the run. And in 2013, Manning set NFL records with 5,477 passing yards and 55 touchdown passes in a single season, many of them on the Drag concept.

• • •

"No matter how many hours you study opponent films," Sid Gillman used to repeat, "there's only going to be eleven players on the other side of the line of scrimmage." It's a simple game, in which strategic beauty comes not from being surprised by some new clever trick but from the sublime, routine brilliance of a master in his element.

WINGING IT

In 1999, Shiloh Christian and Junction City played in the third round of the Arkansas high school football class AA playoffs. Shiloh quickly fell behind 24–0, then 38–14 but rallied to win 70–64 on a touchdown in the final two minutes. The next morning, an Arkansas newspaper called the game "legendary," "mythical," and "unbelievable," prophesying that it would "become one of those games that started with 6,000 in attendance and, as the story grows through the years, will probably end up with around 40,000 there."

Gus Malzahn, then Shiloh Christian's head coach and currently the head man at Auburn, vividly remembers the game. "It was the wildest experience of my coaching career," Malzahn wrote in his book, *The Hurry-Up, No-Huddle: An Offensive Philosophy*. "The first question that will probably come to your mind is, 'Just how bad were both defenses?' The funny thing is that, coming into the game, both teams were undefeated. Junction City was only giving up four points per game, and we were only giving up eleven."

The game started portentously when, just before kickoff, a car backed into a telephone pole, exploding a transformer and knocking out the power. "The game started an hour and a half late, and the scoreboard didn't work, which upset me," Malzahn wrote. "Little did I know, however, that the malfunctioning scoreboard would be an advantage for us when we got so far behind early and our kids couldn't see the score."

Junction City's star running back, Marcus Godfrey, exploded out of the gate for first-quarter touchdown runs of 39, 93, and 79 yards. "I looked at my defensive coordinator, Kevin Johnson, and said, 'They're going to score a hundred points, and he is going to run for a thousand yards.' He looked back at me with a blank expression," Malzahn wrote. "We were in a state of shock."

The ugly start proved to be an opportunity for Malzahn, who believes his wide-open hurry-up system is designed to physically and mentally wear down opponents. When better to test that belief than in a game that looked hopeless? Shiloh narrowed the gap to 51–35 at halftime, and though his team still trailed by a considerable margin, Malzahn knew the tide had turned.

"As I watched their players leaving the field, I noticed some of their athletes were jogging slowly, while others were walking laboriously to their dressing room," Malzahn wrote. "I told our coaches, 'We are going to win this game.'"

He was right, and not for the last time. Malzahn and his madcap offense are the primary reasons why the Tigers have gone from being a last-place SEC West team the year before Malzahn became head coach to a national title contender. Auburn's offensive resurgence has largely stemmed from two factors: the lessons of a thirty-year-old book about a fifty-year-old offense, and the ability of a former high school coach to adapt schemes to his players.

•••

Malzahn began his coaching career in 1991 as a defensive co-ordinator at Hughes High School in Arkansas. After just one season, he was promoted to head coach. "I didn't have a clue what I was doing," Malzahn told *Sports Illustrated* in 2010. "No, I'm serious. I really didn't."

Malzahn had never been in charge of an offense before. Searching for help, he turned to a book famous in coaching circles, *The Delaware Wing-T: An Order of Football*, by Harold "Tubby" Raymond, and followed it "word for word."

The genius of Raymond's book is that it's not merely a collection of football plays, though there's still plenty of that. Instead, it's primarily a treatise on how to think about offensive football. "The Wing-T is more than a formation," Raymond wrote. "It is sequence football." The animating idea behind Raymond's Delaware Wing-T was his belief that the best offenses were built around a tightly wound collection of plays that fit together so that defenses effectively dictated the next play; each time a team tries to stop one thing, it opens itself up to something else. Beginning in the 1950s and lasting into the early 2000s—first as an assistant under Wing-T innovator David Nelson, then as head coach from the mid-1960s on—Raymond fielded teams that devastated defenses. If the opposition tried to stop his base plays, Raymond had counters to his counters, counters to his counters to his counters, and so on. He amplified this sequential approach by "utilizing the misdirection theme to its fullest." With a dizzying array of motions, backfield actions, and fakes, Raymond correctly determined that defenses wouldn't be able to stop his offense if they couldn't find the ball.

Although Malzahn's early teams ran Raymond's brand of the Wing-T verbatim, Malzahn soon began experimenting with the new trends sweeping across football in the 1990s. By the time Shiloh Christian faced Junction City in 1999, Malzahn's offense had evolved into the up-tempo spread that would become his trademark. Raymond's influence remains crucial to Malzahn's offense, however, and much of Auburn's current playbook consists of updated takes on staple Wing-T plays.

In Raymond's Wing-T, wingbacks, receivers, and running backs often went in motion one way or another, and the quarterback almost always carried out one, two, or sometimes even three fakes on a given play. The same is true in Auburn's offense, as Malzahn combines Wing-T plays like the Buck Sweep—which features pulling guards who lead the runner to the outside—with modern fakes and misdirection.

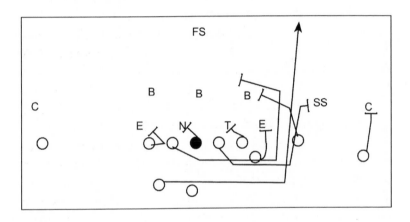

But over the last several seasons, Malzahn and Rhett Lashlee, his offensive coordinator, have evolved the offense beyond its pure Wing-T roots. Yet rather than chase the latest trends floating around coaching clinics, however, the two have always built their offense around their players, in particular their quarterback. While many consider Malzahn a run-game guru, he has coached pass-happy offenses, run-heavy attacks, and evenly balanced offenses over the years.

Following a turbulent season as Arkansas's offensive coordinator under Houston Nutt in 2006, Malzahn became co-offensive coordinator at Tulsa along with Herb Hand, currently the offensive-line coach at Penn State. Tulsa led the country in total offense in both of Malzahn's two seasons, sporting a slightly different style each time. In 2007, Tulsa finished third in the nation in passing offense, as quarterback Paul Smith threw for more than 5,000 yards and 47 touchdowns. The next season, Tulsa finished fifth in rushing, as Malzahn merged his Wing-T-infused run game with the zone-read ideas Hand brought from West Virginia, where he'd coached under Rich Rodriguez. Auburn was fairly balanced in both of Malzahn's first two years as the Tigers' offensive coordinator and coached two very different quarterbacks in Chris Todd (2009) and Cam Newton (2010). And in 2012 white head coach at Arkansas State, QB Ryan Aplin threw for more than 3,200 yards.

In 2013, Auburn was anything but balanced—not that it mattered. The 2013 Tigers, who finished the season 12–2 were the first SEC team to average more than 300 yards rushing per game in almost thirty years. (The last team to do that? The 1985 Auburn team led by Bo Jackson.) But while Newton and Auburn quarterback Nick Marshall both ran for more than 1,000 yards in Malzahn's offense, they did so while using very different approaches. At six foot six and 250 pounds, Newton was essentially Auburn's power back, and Malzahn featured him on a variety of inside runs. Marshall, by contrast, is shorter and lankier than Newton but boasts great quickness and acceleration. As a result, Auburn's 2013 and 2014 offenses focused less on the core Wing-T run plays and more on zone-reads to get Marshall on the edges which gave his running backs, particularly the shifty Tre Mason, space to use vision and patience to find running lanes.

The backbone of Auburn's rushing attack since Malzahn's return has been an amped-up version of the zone-read, which gives Marshall as many as four options: (1) throw a receiver screen, (2) hand it to the running back, (3) keep the ball, or (4) keep the ball and then toss it to a receiver who can sit in an open area of the defense if the man covering him comes up for the run—a form of the quadruple option.

Auburn used a version of this play repeatedly on its final offensive drive against Alabama in the 2014 Iron Bowl, including when Marshall hit receiver Sammie Coates for the game-tying touchdown as the entire Tide defense collapsed on the quarterback.

The most dangerous wrinkle in Auburn's offense in 2013 and 2014, however, was providing the QB with more protection when he kept the ball. As the zone-read has become increasingly popular over the last several years, defenses have devised a variety of ways to defend it, often by confusing and overwhelming the quarterback.

Malzahn and Lashlee have countered those defensive responses by borrowing the bluff concept from Chris Ault's Nevada attack: using tight ends, H-backs, and fullbacks to arc-block linebackers and safeties who crash when the quarterback keeps the ball on the zone-read. Below is a diagram of "Indy Dash," Malzahn's term for the inside zone with an arc block.

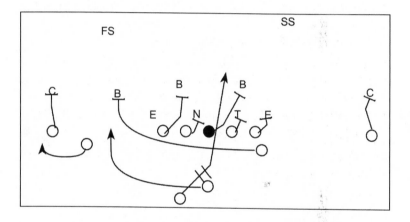

Although Marshall running the shotgun zone-read is far afield from the old-school Wing-T, these subtle adjustments are pure Raymond. They're sequenced plays, in which the base play sets up the counter, and the counter sets up the counter to the counter, all dressed up with misdirection.

• • •

Current Auburn offensive coordinator Lashlee was Malzahn's quarterback at Shiloh back in 1999. Trailing 64–62 with roughly two minutes left in the fourth quarter, the then-sophomore—who set a national record with 672 passing yards that day—threw a touchdown pass to the back left corner. Along with the two-point conversion, it put Shiloh ahead for good.

Malzahn still cites that game as the best embodiment of all the reasons why he believes in his offensive philosophy. "Quite obviously," Malzahn said, "we wouldn't have won the game or the state championship that year" if the coaches and staff didn't also believe in that philosophy—or in Malzahn himself.

But no one should have been surprised. Whether it's Shiloh vs. Junction, Auburn's Cam Newton led national championship in 2010, or the "Kick Six" missed field goal return to beat Alabama in 2013, miracles seem to follow Malzahn wherever he goes. Just ask the six thousand—or forty thousand—fans who watched a pretty spectacular high school football game in northwest Arkansas in 1999. They know that Malzahn's teams are capable of anything.

MONSTER MASH

Coaches and quarterbacks nowadays are exceptional at identifying and exploiting defensive weaknesses. Defenses now, with the rise of spread offenses, often give away their soft spots by how they line up, and the myriad of reads, packaged plays, and options make exploiting those weaknesses ever-simpler stuff.

But football is a game of give and take, and defenses are responding. And they are reacting to the up-tempo, read-on-the-run offenses of today in two main ways. First, becoming more flexible, with more hybrid-type defenders such as "big nickel" safety/linebacker hybrids who can blitz, stuff the run or drop into coverage. And, second, they are increasingly doing more of their own attacking.

The key for defenses is to attack, but to attack intelligently. Offenses will exploit obvious weaknesses, so the best approach is to combine aggressive tactics with sound schemes and to set traps for offenses. And one of the best—and oldest—methods for doing that is to combine an overload blitz with angle stunts that go the opposite direction. This tactic is increasingly popular at every level of football, particularly against nouveau-spread attacks, but it has old, old roots.

The combination of overload blitzes to one side with angle stunts going the other way was a feature of one of football's most dominating defenses, the 5–2 "Monster." In the old 5–2 Monster defense, which dominated offenses in the middle of the last century, the defense aligned with five defensive linemen, two linebackers, and a "monster" defender who lined up either to the wide side of the field or to the strength of the offense, typically the latter. With a nose guard lined up directly over the center, the defense had three additional defenders lined up to the offense's left and four additional ones to the offense's right. This gave the defense the chance to overpower offenses to their strength side, where they typically liked to run to.

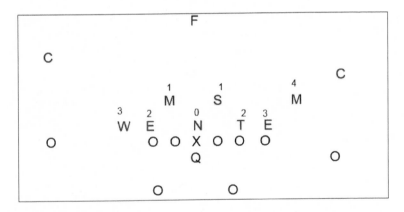

But as the defense evolved over time, this increasingly became a trap for the offense. Against the 5–2 Monster, offenses typically called plays that attacked the weak side of their formation. Much of the modern run game is simply about identifying where the extra defenders are and running away from them, and running away from the monster seemed as good a plan as any.

Except it was exactly what the defense wanted the offense to do. The reason was because most of those 5–2 Monster teams, despite lining up with extra players to one side versus the other, used angle stunts (*i.e.*, defensive-line movements) away from the monster player. The net result was that the 5–2 Monster was a *balanced defense*.

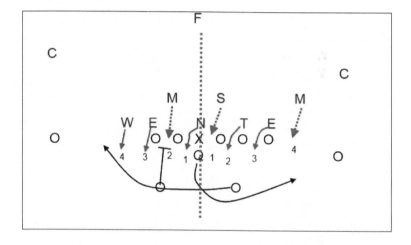

Thus the monster's great success—and it was one of the most popular defenses in football for at least thirty years—was as much about psychology as it was schematics; there were unbalanced defenses, and there were balanced defenses, but looked like one while actually being the other. Against balanced defenses, the offense wants to run to its strength or to the tight end. Against unbalanced defenses, offenses want to run wherever they have a numbers advantage, typically to the weak side. The monster wreaked havoc with that kind of calculus.

• • •

While no team uses the pure 5–2 Monster anymore (except in goal-line situations), defensive coaches have not forgotten its lessons and instead apply them every week across football. It's just a matter of adaptation.

The first change is philosophical. While the 5–2 Monster was primarily a run-stuffing defense, and the overload combined with an angle stunt was meant to play games with run plays, the modern approach typically begins by attacking pass-protection schemes. With the rise of spread formations the most popular pass-protection concept has been six-man pass-protection with the five offensive linemen and one running back.

In the older, true West Coast offense pass-protection schemes, the most common six-man pass protections required an offensive lineman, typically a guard or sometimes the center, to "dual read," meaning he had to first look to one potential blitzer, and if he did not rush the quarterback, then the blocker was responsible for a different defender. Dual reading by offensive linemen has largely faded from football in recent years due, primarily, to increasingly effective zone blitzes and the physical demands it places on linemen. It's very difficult to ask an offensive lineman to read an interior blitzer and then, if he doesn't rush, peel out to block a linebacker or defensive back. More than likely, even if the lineman reads it perfectly, he will not get there to make the block.

But dual reading is still necessary because offenses still need the ability to get all five potential receivers out into a pass route if the defense only rushes three or four defenders. So dual reading is now increasingly handled by running backs who are better positioned both to see which defender is blitzing and to react in time to make the block. With a running back dual reading, offenses typically use slide or gap pass protection away from the back, with the running back responsible for either of two potential blitzers. If only one or the other rushes, the running back blocks; if neither rushes, the running back runs a pass route; if they both blitz, the quarterback must see that and get the ball out of his hands quickly.

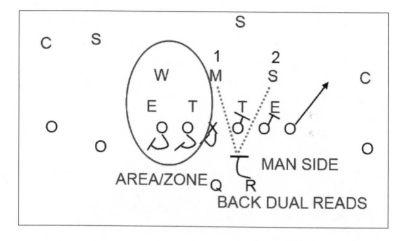

But if defensive coaches identify a dual reading running back, they have tactics of their own. In particular, defenses might blitz both of the defenders the running back is responsible for while dropping other defenders into coverage—in short, an overload tactic. It's extremely common now for defenses to set their overload blitz by directing it to the side where the running back is lined up, presenting a rather dangerous quandary for that running back.

And making this tactic even more effective is the enduring lesson of the monster: an overload blitz combined with an angle stunt *going the other way*. And why is that so important, particularly versus spread attacks? On most shotgun-spread running plays, the running back runs to the side *away* from where he lined up, while the quarterback reads the back side. The back side blitzers in this scheme are taught to read through the running back to the quarterback, so if it is a zone-read play, they can account for the quarterback. Indeed, if the quarterback pulls the ball on a keeper, he should run directly into two blitzing defenders.

But if he gives the ball to the running back, the defense is well positioned to stop the run play to that side as well, as the rest of the defense is running their angle stunt in that direction and thus are likely to penetrate and potentially get a tackle for loss. And this tactic doesn't only work with zone blitzes. It also works with man-to-man coverage, as shown in a page from Rex Ryan's playbook from when he was head coach of the New York Jets.

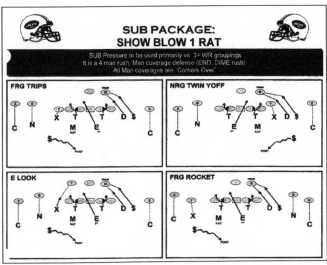

These blitzes show an overload blitz directly at the hapless running back, combined with angle stunts in the opposite direction, to balance the defense and take away run plays away from the blitzers. And Ryan takes it a step further. In the above blitzes, he's trying to get an overload blitz—where the offense cannot account for an extra rusher—while only rushing four defenders! It's good stuff.

Of course there are counters for offenses, or at least tactics to throw a defense off the scent. They primarily involve playing games with the alignment of the running back by motioning or shifting him back and forth just before the snap, or lining him up to one side and giving him pass-protection responsibilities to the other. Unredictability remains crucial in football. But the overload and angle stunts are powerful weapons in every defensive coach's arsenal. Offenses can't have all the fun.

THE ARCHITECT: HOW ART BRILES BUILT BAYLOR

The season before Art Briles's arrival was more of the same for Baylor. In 2007, the fifth year under Guy Morriss, Baylor went 3–9—good for its customary last-place finish in the Big 12 South. Since the first football game of Big 12 play, in 1996, the Bears had finished sixth on their side of the conference eleven times. The last time they'd been to a bowl, the Big 12 conference didn't exist. The only time of the year Baylor was relevant in college football was when the other schools in the conference wanted to schedule their homecoming games.

Seven years later, Briles has turned Baylor football into the state of Texas's answer to the Oregon Ducks: fast players, fast tempo, and even faster scoring, all infused with a long drawl and a gunslinger's mind-set. Over the past four seasons, Baylor—a fifteen-thousand-student private school in Waco—has gone 40-12 behind some of the best offenses in football, and it has done it with a revolving cast of players. Led by Heisman Trophy winner Robert Griffin III, Baylor won ten games in 2011 and finished second in the nation in total offense. In 2012, after losing Griffin to the NFL, as well as their leading receiver and rusher, the Bears finished second nationally in total offense, upset the number-two team in the country, and crushed UCLA 49–26 in the Holiday Bowl. Before the 2013 season, Baylor again lost its quarterback and leading receiver to graduation. And with Bryce Petty at quarterback, Baylor won back-to-back Big 12 titles while averaging 52 and 48 points per game in 2013 and 2014, respectively. All of this has happened at a program that, before the 2010 season, hadn't gone to a bowl game in fifteen years.

Briles has made believers out of players and fans conditioned by years of disappointment by having the audacity to expect success at a place that has never really known it. If this weren't happening at Baylor, Briles's approach would be something like arrogance: we are going to score, and we are going to win. "We do not try to go to the body to set up the knockout shot," Briles said at a lecture for high school coaches. "We try to score on every snap."

That Baylor, an afterthought for thirty years, can approach football like this speaks to what Briles has built during his tenure. There have been many contributors to Baylor's recent success, not least of all Griffin—but the architect of the turnaround is the Bears' head coach, just as he's been at so many stops before. Briles has made a career of building winners by lighting up scoreboards, and Baylor is his best job yet.

• • •

Ten QBs who started games in the NFL in the 2013 season played high school football in Texas. Some of this may just be a lucky run, but it's also not a surprise. After decades of grind-it-out power football, the Texas high school game has gone the opposite direction—fully embracing the trend of wide-open, up-tempo spread offenses. In Texas, most high school quarterbacks practice passing year-round: Fall practice is buttressed by spring practice, and whatever offseason remains is spent visiting innumerable passing camps or playing in seven-on-seven passing leagues. When the fall games do begin, they resemble those pass-only workouts more than ever.

Arguably, no coach did more to lead the way for these wide-open attacks than Briles, first as head coach at Hamlin High School and later at Stephenville. Briles's teams ran the spread offense back in the 1980s and 1990s, long before it was popular in college or the NFL. Most important, they won with that offense. Before Briles's arrival in 1988, Stephenville's football team had not made the Texas state playoffs since 1952. Briles won four state championships in a seven-year span, and his 1998 championship squad set a national record for total offense in a single season with a staggering 8,664 yards.

Briles played college football at the University of Houston for the legendary Bill Yeoman, the creator of the vaunted "Houston Veer" triple option. As a young coach, Briles used Yeoman's scheme, but he quickly decided a change was needed to beat the more talented teams in Texas.

"What I looked for was an edge, something different. So in '85 we went to the one-back, four wides and went 14–1," Briles told SBNation.com. "At Stephenville, we definitely had to do something that gave ourselves a chance to get the opportunity to win football games. We weren't just gonna line up and beat people. We had to be a little unconventional, which we were."

Briles's success as a high school coach got him his first college coaching job, as Mike Leach's running backs coach at

Texas Tech in 2000. He stayed in Lubbock for three seasons before getting an offer to take over as head coach of a moribund University of Houston program in 2003. It was not a glamour job. According to Briles, he was the lowest-paid coach in Division I football. In 2001, two years before Briles's arrival, the Cougars had gone 0–11. Yet Houston went to a bowl game in four of Briles's five seasons, which included a ten-win campaign in 2006.

At Stephenville and Houston, Briles earned a reputation as a motivator and as a coach for whom players loved to play. His ability to articulate a vision for his program, even in the darkest of times, is why he has been able to surround himself with good players, good coaches, and good people at every stop. There's no question, though, that it's Briles's offense—which has averaged 600 yards of offense per game since 2013—that is the engine of Baylor's success and the source for much of the optimism surrounding his program. When Baylor's offense is rolling—when the aggressive plays, speedy weapons, and up-tempo pace work in unison—the offense is less about executing football plays and more about waging psychological warfare.

Two weeks removed from Baylor's 73-point, 872-yard thrashing of West Virginia in 2013, WVU's then-defensive coordinator Keith Patterson was still describing the loss as "unlike anything I've ever been associated with in my entire life. It was just catastrophic in a lot of ways to our psyche." When Baylor scores 35 in a quarter, 50 in a half, or 70 in a game, it's hard for the opposing team to recover mentally—not just in that game, but for the rest of their season. The fact that it's Baylor—yesterday's footstool—is not lost on anyone, either.

Ask any offensive-minded football coach how he plans to attack a defense and at some point—maybe after talking about establishing the run, or about getting the ball to his best players—he'll say that his offense is designed to stretch the defense horizontally and vertically. The idea of using the entire field has long been part of basic football theory, but most offenses don't follow through on that promise. They may toss in the occasional downfield throw, or a sweep or short pass to the flat, before receding back into something pedestrian and predictable. Many of the now-ubiquitous spread offenses are better defined by their uniformity than their uniqueness, as every team tries to sprinkle some Oregon spread or Nevada pistol into their game plans; nowadays it seems everyone is trying to be different in the exact same ways.

Then there's Baylor. Superficially, Baylor is yet another shotgun spread that pushes the tempo and rarely huddles. But when you watch the Bears, it's evident that this is an offense unlike the others. While more and more college and NFL teams are adopting the same up-tempo spread philosophy Briles used at Stephenville, Baylor has stayed one step ahead by taking these ideas—from formations to play-calling aggressiveness to pace—to their extremes.

$$\cdots$$

The first thing to notice when watching Baylor is the splits of the wide receivers. While most teams put their wide receivers on the numbers, the Bears line theirs up well outside, sometimes directly on the sideline. By doing this, they force defenses to account for the entire width of the field. The fascinating advantage of Baylor's splits is the effect they have on pass coverage. Defenses now use lots of complex, hybrid pass coverages, but most still reduce to a basic distinction: Is it man-to-man or zone? By taking such wide splits, Baylor puts every pass defender on an island, transforming most zone defenses into de facto one-on-one man coverage.

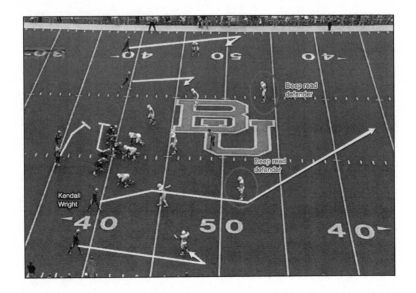

For example, if a defense tries to cover the slot receivers with a safety, such as with Quarters coverage or any kind of man-to-man, Briles loves to send his speedy slot receivers deep against the often slower-footed safety. No team goes deep to its slot receivers more than Baylor, and few go deep as often, period.

The beneficiary of the wide receiver splits and the deep shots is Baylor's running game. Briles and his staff are committed to the running game, and Baylor has averaged over 215 yards rushing per game over each of the past four seasons, and Briles's experience with Yeoman's veer has helped Baylor's have a more diverse run game than most other spread offenses.

But what really makes Baylor's run game go is that every run has built-in passes, and not just screens, either. According to Briles, Baylor has "a lot of different reads off every one of our plays for our quarterback," and Pat Narduzzi, who studied Baylor in depth before facing them in the 2015 Cotton Bowl explained that, "with Baylor, every run is a pass and every pass is a run."

In the example above, Briles combined three plays in one: (1) a quick receiver screen to the QB's right, (2) an inside run with a lead blocker, and (3) a post route by the receiver to the QB's left. If the defense fails to put enough defenders out wide to cover the screen, the QB can flip the ball to the perimeter for an easy few yards. But the QC is actually deciding whether to hand off or throw the post *after* the snap, as he reads the weak safety—the "goat," in Baylor's terminology. If the safety hangs back, the QB simply hands the ball off, but if he flies up for the run, the QB pulls the ball out and rifles the ball to the receiver for a big play. It's pretty stuff, besides being brutally difficult to stop. Just ask their opponents.

"Every time the quarterback rides that tailback, he's got a downfield route, he's got options," explained Narduzzi. "Some people do that, but [Baylor] does it more than anybody in the country. Everything is built in. I would say of their passing game, probably 50% is all built into the run play. There's going to be run/pass conflicts for your defensive players. That's what's special about what they do. You look at it and you go, 'Wow.'"

The beauty of Baylor's offense is that it's almost all driven by structure and repetition rather than complexity. When

Baylor runs a pure play-action pass (as opposed to a packaged play), it typically uses just one of three routes for its outside receivers: a go or vertical route, a post, or a comeback. That's it. It works because Baylor calls play action when the safeties can't help—or be helped—and it's almost impossible to simultaneously defend the threat of all three of those routes at the same time. For truly great offenses, it's never the cleverness of the plays or concepts individually. It's how the entire offense fits together.

Finally, Baylor takes those perfectly aligned pieces and supercharges them with a tempo most teams can't match. The speed forces Baylor's opponents to show their hands; defenses can't shift and disguise if the ball might be snapped at any moment. In Baylor's case, the up-tempo no-huddle is not just a tactic, it's central to its very identity.

"The biggest thing in the success of our offense is the tempo at which we played," explained Briles. "I want to be the fastest team in America as far as the number of times we snap the ball. People do not pay money to come to a game and watch a slowdown offense. If they go to the restroom, I want them to come back and say, 'What happened while I was gone?' They will miss something if they leave the game. When we have the ball, we will do something with it. You only get twelve possessions a game, and we want to get our money's worth."

Baylor's offense (and an improved defense) has made the Bears national-title contenders as they narrowly missed the college football playoff in 2014, but with success comes attention, not only in Texas but throughout the country. In the summer of 2013, while speaking to a gathering of Texas high school coaches, former Texas head coach Mack Brown was asked how to stop Baylor. Mack shrugged before saying, "I mean, nobody stops Baylor."

THE GREAT DEFENDER

In the days leading up to Super Bowl XXV, then-New York Giants defensive coordinator Bill Belichick was searching for any weakness the opposing Buffalo Bills might possess. Powered by four future Hall of Famers, Buffalo's "K-Gun" offense had led the NFL in scoring during the 1990 season and had already posted 44 and 51 points in the playoffs against the Dolphins and Raiders.

But Belichick eventually settled on an edge he thought he could exploit. His first job in the NFL had been under the K-Gun's architect, Buffalo offensive coordinator Ted Marchibroda. While head coach of the Baltimore Colts in 1975, Marchibroda had hired Belichick for a barely paid gig analyzing game film, and the two remained friendly. But this was business, not personal, and Belichick knew that the old-school Marchibroda, though a great tactician, would have trained his quarterbacks the same way he'd once trained his junior film guy: by filling them up with knowledge and then handing them the reins. Analysts wondered how Buffalo's no-huddle attack could play so fast, but Belichick knew that Marchibroda was forged in an era when quarterbacks like Bart Starr and Johnny Unitas called their own plays, and that Bills passer Jim Kelly had the same freedom.

That knowledge was all Belichick needed. Later, Belichick would tell author David Halberstam he didn't think Kelly read defenses as well as some other NFL quarterbacks did, which made Belichick confident he could stay one step ahead. While Marchibroda would be able to explain the Giants' looks to Kelly between series, during them Kelly would have to match wits with Belichick unaided. With each drive, Belichick made sure to appear to show Kelly exactly what he'd seen in the prior series, while in reality making subtle but crucial tweaks, such as replacing a defensive back with a linebacker or changing a single defender's coverage responsibility to set a trap. Belichick amplified the effect by working out of an unusual dime defense featuring six defensive backs, two traditional defensive linemen, and three linebackers (including Lawrence Taylor) to better defend Buffalo's talented receivers.

It worked. The Giants held Kelly and his receivers in check en route to a 20–19 win, albeit with some help from one of the most infamous missed field goals in NFL history, and today Belichick's Super Bowl XXV game plan sits in the Pro Football Hall of Fame. Already well known at the time in coaching circles, Belichick became a household name by relying on two of the pillars that continue to define him: ingenious defensive tactics and precision without sentimentality.

Twenty-four years later, head coach Bill Belichick is still bombarding opponents with shrewd, coldly rational tactics. The result: his Patriots just claimed their fourth championship of his reign. In winning Super Bowl XLIX, Belichick's team had to defeat a team coached by the NFL's other best defensive coach, Pete Carroll. But while Carroll's otherworldly defenses have succeeded the last few seasons largely because of the way Carroll elegantly uses simplicity to unleash his squad's great talent, Belichick resists classification. No modern football coach can match Belichick's deep knowledge of schemes and strategies, or his multidecade track record of applying that knowledge to devastating effect.

• • •

Most successful coaches can point to one or two key mentors or influencers who shaped their thinking. But while Belichick has worked with coaches like Marchibroda, Bill Parcells, and Ray Perkins, and he identifies the men who shaped him as "a menagerie,"‡ one figure stands out: "My dad, that was a constant."

Belichick's father, Steve, might be the greatest "scout" in football history, at least based on how the term was used in the 1940s, '50s, and '60s. Today, a typical football scout focuses almost entirely on evaluating personnel, like potential draft picks or free-agent signees; in contrast, Steve was an extension of the coaching staffs at Vanderbilt, North Carolina, and particularly Navy, where he worked for more than thirty years for seven head coaches, traveling to watch and analyze opponents' games in person.

Accurately evaluating game film is hard enough for today's coaches and scouts, who benefit from rewindable All-22 digital game footage; accurately charting and analyzing a team's personnel, formations, shifts, plays, and tendencies *in real time* as well as Steve did is almost inconceivable. He was revered for

---

‡ Belichick has even credited his high school coach, sharing his philosophy with Halberstam: "The coach was king, and had been king in the past, and was going to be king in the future." Sound familiar?

his ability to recognize patterns and spot things no one else noticed, and he compiled his thoughts into lengthy reports that he delivered each week to his head coach, which also became his son's introduction to the game within the game.

According to Halberstam's book on Belichick, *The Education of a Coach*, a nine-year-old Belichick made a deal with his father. If he finished his homework early, the old scout would give his son a preview of that week's report, allowing the youngster to gorge himself on play diagrams and digressions on the popular tactics of the era, like the single wing and straight T-formation offenses and the wide-tackle six and gap-eight defenses. Halberstam noted that Belichick quickly became conversant in football arcana, eloquently explaining to one old coach at ten years old that he should switch to an Oklahoma 5–2 (a predecessor to today's 3–4 defenses and a cousin of the 5-2 Monster) to better match up against an upcoming opponent. Around that time, meanwhile, Steve cemented his legacy as one of the greatest scouts of his era by publishing *Football Scouting Methods*, a treatise on the art of scouting. (The book was recently republished, and the publisher's description includes this ringing endorsement: "Bill Belichick's use of these methods led to the 2007 National Football League videotaping controversy, widely dubbed 'Spygate.'")

By the time Belichick got his first NFL job under Marchibroda at the age of 23, he was already something of a football historian, intimately aware of football tactics and their evolutions. The young scholar soon realized he had a knack for applying that knowledge on the field, quickly rising from an assistant who earned $25 a week to defensive coordinator of the New York Giants by age 33. While his father was more of a football theorist, Belichick's forte has always been applied knowledge.

But his father's influence remained, and Belichick has never stopped learning. He's renowned for spending his summers picking the brains of coaches he respects in search of anything he might find useful, which is why, despite having risen through the ranks almost exclusively as a defensive coach, Belichick is also an offensive master. The Patriots have repeatedly stayed ahead of the curve, going to shotgun-spread and no-huddle attacks before the rest of the league, then going back to extra tight ends, fullbacks, and linemen while the rest of the league turned to the spread.

The players know who drives these shifts. A few years ago, after yet another parade of offensive assistants had left for bigger jobs, Tom Brady confidently remarked to ESPN that "as long as we have Belichick, I always think that we're going to be just fine." So far, he's been right.

• • •

Still, Belichick's hallmark remains his defense, and the way that unit plays is what opposing coaches most admire. "There's very few coaches that I steal from, but Bill Belichick is one of them," Buffalo head coach Rex Ryan has said. "So creative what he does coverage-wise, how he looks at things, puts traps out there. The guy is an amazing coach. Best coach in football—it's not even close. That's a guy I will study."

Unlike the many coaches who identify with a particular style or tree, Belichick isn't locked into a singular ideology. He seems to effortlessly shift between tactics from week to week, and he's always bristled at attempts to neatly characterize his defenses, once calling the notion that he prefers a 3–4 defense a "media fabrication." For Belichick, there are no pure defensive systems, only objectives and constraints and a hyperrational evaluation of each. "You decide defensively how you want to defend them in the running game. Do you want to defend them with gap control? Do you want to two-gap? Do you want to try to overload the box with extra guys and play eight against seven or seven against six? Those are all the choices you make. With every decision, there's going to be an upside, there's going to be a downside. There will be advantages to playing certain things, there will be disadvantages." This is the kind of multitiered thought process Belichick calls "pretty straightforward." Right.

Thanks to that mentality, Belichick's greatness has never stemmed from the Big Idea, unless the big idea is the relentless application of many little ideas. For example: With the Giants, one of Belichick's best tactics was something he called BTF, or blitz the formation, an idea he gleaned from Buddy Ryan's famed 46 defense with the Chicago Bears. Instead of calling for specific players to blitz the quarterback, Belichick would make a BTF call, and once the offense showed how it was lining up, his players would check to a specialty blitz designed for when that particular opponent used that particular formation. In recent years, however, Belichick has expanded on this idea by having his players adjust their blitz assignments not only based on the offense's formation, but by having them trade assignments after the play begins.

On most NFL passing plays, the center is usually the key to understanding how the offense is trying to protect the quarterback. Defenses prefer to rush away from the center, which creates a mismatch in favor of the defense by forcing the running back to block a blitzing NFL linebacker (and also eliminates a potential receiver out of the backfield). If the running back isn't staying in to block, or if he is but whiffs, the defense has an unblocked blitzer, which is even better.

Today's offenses are nimble enough to redirect their pass-protection schemes toward the most likely blitzers at the line. Belichick, however, enables his defenders to regain the advantage by teaching them to read the offense, specifically the center. For example, Belichick frequently calls blitzes with potential rushers lined up to the offense's left and right, with each reading the center's movement. If the center slides toward the keyed defender, he drops into coverage, and if the center slides away from the keyed defender, he turns kamikaze and blitzes the quarterback. Here's a page describing this tactic, called "Rain," from the playbook of one of Belichick's former assistants, Alabama head coach Nick Saban:

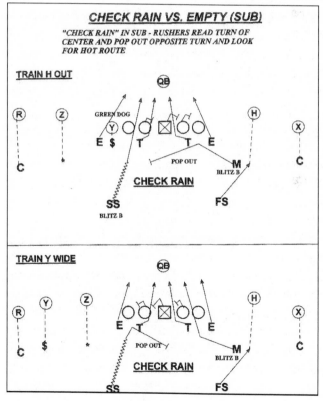

In week 16 of the 2014 season, with the Patriots cling-
ing to a 17–16 lead with just more than six minutes left,
the New York Jets faced third-and-4 from New England's
24-yard line. Just before the snap, New England's entire defensive front shifted, as defensive tackles Vince Wilfork and
Chris Jones moved inside, and linebackers Jamie Collins and
Dont'a Hightower—the defenders Belichick had designated
for a tag-team Rain blitz—moved just outside the tackles. As
the play began, New York's center slid to his left, so Collins
dropped back, right into Geno Smith's throwing lane, while
Hightower flew into the backfield and sacked Smith for a ten-
yard loss.

With the ball pushed back, Wilfork blocked Nick Folk's
52-yard field-goal attempt, the Jets failed to threaten to score
again, and Belichick notched another victory, once again subtly
and masterfully upending his opponent.

• • •

It's hard to win in the NFL, where most games are decided by
small, often-overlooked moments. The great coaches, however,
are adept at finding and exploiting seemingly infinitesimal
advantages. There's a reason Bill Walsh called his book *Finding
the Winning Edge* and Don Shula called his *The Winning Edge*:
gaining an "edge" is often the difference between winning and
losing. One doesn't steward his team to twelve consecutive
ten-plus-win seasons, as Belichick has, without an uncanny
ability to identify and exploit the on-field edges that add up
to wins.

But what about edges off the field? It's impossible to write
about Belichick without raising the question. Like almost all
of his peers, Belichick isn't above a little gamesmanship if it

might help him win. According to Halberstam, in order to slow down Buffalo's no-huddle offense in Super Bowl XXV, Belichick told his Giants players to "accidentally kick the ball" away from the officials after it had been set up for play.

But there's a difference between gamesmanship and breaking the rules. We all know about Spygate, and Deflategate has dominated headlines since the story broke in January 2015. Considering it's about whether someone intentionally took air out of some footballs, it's easy to say the story's magnitude would have been considerably less had it not involved the Patriots and Belichick. That's not to minimize the allegations—rules are rules, and the report by Ted Wells commissioned by the NFL found that Patriots staffers were more likely than not to have tampered with the footballs' air pressure—but instead to say that the idea of the Patriots surreptitiously leaking air out of footballs to try to gain an advantage for the Patriots perfectly matches the popular narrative of the Belichick-era Patriots as willing to do anything to get an edge. In fact, for many, Belichick's defense that he'd never really thought about the air pressure of a football during his forty years of coaching was the most unbelievable part of this entire saga. Belichick thinks of everything.

• • •

Every generation seems to get the football coaches it deserves. In the postwar decades, leading coaches like Paul Brown, Vince Lombardi, and Woody Hayes were imperial figures defined by discipline and a militaristic approach to the game. In his book, the elder Belichick made sure to always refer to the leader of Navy's chief rival, legendary Army coach Earl Blaik, as "Colonel Blaik." Nowadays, most NFL coaches are company men, professionals who started as trainees and made their way up to corner offices by working hard and "managing up" the same way they would have at General Electric or Goldman Sachs.

The exception, as always, is Belichick. Compared to his peers, he's far less polished (David Letterman once said he looked like a "Sherpa guide") and far less concerned with sentiment (Parcells used to refer to him as "Gloom"). But he's also more knowledgeable, more rational, and more exacting. Belichick is a grim, calculating technocrat. But he's also the best coach we have.

ACKNOWLEDGMENTS

I am extremely indebted to many people for their help and inspiration, none more so than my wife, Sarah, who, in addition to patiently listening to me drone on about whatever new idea or piece it is I'm working on, has always provided me with excellent feedback and support. I'd like to thank B. Radcliff Menge for reading a draft of the manuscript and providing invaluable edits and perspective (which resulted in me making more edits to the manuscript than I think he—or I—had anticipated). And I am tremendously grateful to the many people at Grantland—Bill Simmons, Dan Fierman, Sean Fennessey, Mallory Rubin, Bill Barnwell, Chris Ryan, Rafe Bartholomew, Robert Mays and many others—who provided me with encouragement, opportunity, guidance and, in the case of much of this book, thoughtful editing. I'm very fortunate to have worked with many talented people in many places throughout my career, none better than the Grantland team.

I'm particularly grateful to the staffs of the Nike Coach of Year Clinics and American Football Coaches Association who provided me with access to treasure troves of material. And, lastly, I'd like to thank the many, many coaches who have spent countless hours explaining some seemingly simple concept to me over and over until I was sure I had it, while putting up with my many, many questions. There would no book—indeed, there be no Smart Football at all—without your kindness and patience.

ABOUT THE AUTHOR

Chris B. Brown is a contributing writer for *ESPN/Grantland* and writes and edits *Smart Football*, which can be found at http://smartfootball.com. He has also written for the *New York Times*, *Yahoo! Sports*, *Slate*, and *Deadspin*. You can also follow him on Twitter at @smartfootball. When not writing about football, Chris practices law.

23693501R00116

Made in the USA
Middletown, DE
31 August 2015